MESSAGES

OF THE THIRD ASSEMBLY

THE LUTHERAN WORLD FEDERATION

MESSAGES

OF THE THIRD ASSEMBLY

THE LUTHERAN WORLD FEDERATION

The opening worship sermon, keynote
address, sub-theme lectures and the resulting theses of the Third Assembly of
the Lutheran World Federation, Minneapolis, Minnesota, Aug. 15-25, 1957.

"Christ Frees and Unites"

AUGSBURG PUBLISHING HOUSE

MINNEAPOLIS   MINNESOTA

MESSAGES
of the Third Assembly
THE LUTHERAN WORLD FEDERATION
Library of Congress Catalog Card No. 57-14826

Manufactured in the United States

Foreword

This volume, *Messages of the Third Assembly,* contains the main results of the 1957 Minneapolis Assembly of the Lutheran World Federation. Without a doubt the great spiritual impact of Bishop Ordass' sermon at the opening service was an important factor in the tone of the Assembly. Therefore it is included. Bishop Hanns Lilje presented the keynote address of the Assembly and was also asked to write a letter to the churches commending the theses presented on the final day.

The 51 theses contained in the final chapter of this book are the result of intensive study, discussion and debate by the delegates and official visitors during the Assembly. The commission on theology had prepared previously a study document which had been distributed widely to pastors and laity well in advance. In addition to this material the six lectures in this book were presented to the Assembly, one on the general theme "Christ Frees and Unites" and one on each of the sub-topics. The discussion group leaders and recorders developed the theses on the basis of the study document, the lectures, the ideas presented in the groups, and the discussion at the plenary sessions. Dr. Franklin Clark Fry, the new president of the LWF, directed the work of the discussion group leaders and the production of the theses. It was also he who originated the new method of handling a theme of this kind. The Assembly received the theses and commended them to the churches for serious study and comment.

It is our hope that the delegates and official visitors will interpret the theses and that pastors and laity will engage in lively, vital debate on the questions raised.

CARL E. LUND-QUIST,
Executive Secretary,
Lutheran World Federation

Contents

Bishop Lajos Ordass

Bishop of the Southern Church District (with his seat in Budapest) and Primate of the Lutheran Church of Hungary, Bishop Ordass was reinstated in ecclesiastical office on Reformation Day, October 31, 1956. He returned to active service in the Church shortly after he was absolved of communist charges which sent him to prison for nearly two years in 1948 and forced him into retirement for six years after his release.

Born in 1901 at Torzsa in the Batschka District (now part of Yugoslavia), he studied theology and history at Budapest and Sopron, Hungary, and at Halle, Germany. He served pastorates in Southern Hungary and Budapest from 1924 through 1937, when he was named "senior" in his district. In 1941 he moved permanently to Budapest, where he distinguished himself in the Church's struggle against the coercive measures of the Hungarian national-socialist government, particularly the nationalization of church schools.

He was elected bishop in 1945, heading the largest Lutheran diocese in the country. In 1947 he was elected a vice president of the Lutheran World Federation at its First Assembly at Lund, Sweden.

The Fruits of the Death of Jesus Christ

Text: John 12:20-26

W E ARE gathered here around our Lord Jesus Christ. In recent years we have witnessed a number of world conferences. These have been held for various reasons and have been attended by people with many motives. The only reason for our meeting here is that we want to be with Jesus Christ.

We are like the disciples described in our text. Their hearts were filled with joy because they could be with their Lord. But they had another reason for rejoicing. They had learned that there were other people who did not know Jesus, but whose hearts were filled with the desire: "We wish to see Jesus."

I should like to dwell for a moment upon this Biblical statement, "We wish to see Jesus." I should like to address this question to each of my friends here: Are we clearly aware of the fact that it was not only these Greeks who were once possessed with the desire to see Jesus Christ, the Son of God, but also our world and countless men today who have this desire? It may

3

be possible that this is not always expressed in clear words. But if we not only listen to human words, but also seek to understand that silent and secret yearning which arises in the hearts of men, then we shall know how many people wish to see Jesus.

In fact, I can go one step farther. In our text Jesus speaks of His death. His words focus our attention upon those persons who opposed Him and drove Him to His death. Jesus invaded their lives, too. Herod was not the only one who wanted to see Jesus. Nor was Saul of Tarsus the only one whom Jesus began to attract while still an enemy, and whom He continued to attract until finally Saul could no longer resist Him and joined His believers with quiet devotion.

I have said this because for all of us there is something encouraging and uplifting in the thought that our gracious Lord can exert so powerful an attraction upon those who appear indifferent and even upon those who are openly hostile toward Him.

God's Holy Spirit arouses in us the question: What is it in Jesus Christ that awakens our love? What is it which creates yearning in the hearts of the uncommitted? What is it which causes even His enemies to surrender?

I find the answer to this question in one of the parables in which Jesus speaks of Himself and which I hold to be the most profound of all the parables which refer to Him.

Here He compares Himself to a grain of wheat.

. . . To a grain of wheat, such as everyone needs to sustain his daily life.

. . . To a grain of wheat, such as God referred to after the Flood: ". . . while the earth remains, seedtime and harvest . . . shall not cease . . . ." (Gen. 8:22).

Just so important is Christ today and in all eternity.

How striking an analogy this is!

Without a doubt there are many of us here who have examined a grain of wheat for its quality during the threshing season, or perhaps who have hulled an ear of wheat and watched the grain roll from one hand into the other. At such times one may have curious thoughts concerning the fate of a grain of wheat.

A grain of wheat may be crushed between millstones. This is the price of its becoming bread for nourishment.

Or it may serve quite a different function. The farmer may take it and, with earnest hope, sow it into the furrow. Thus it will bear fruit for the future.

But the ultimate fate of the grain of wheat is always death. This is why Christ compares Himself with the grain of wheat.

He came to die.

If we look at the life of Jesus from the human point of view we see that—just like the grain of wheat between the millstones—He died a violent death.

But if, following the Bible, we look at the life of Jesus from God's point of view, then we see it quite differently. We see that God—the supreme Master of the world—sowed His Son, the Christ, and allowed Him to die so that His death might bear much fruit for life eternal.

Jesus knew this and deliberately allowed Himself to be put to death so that this death might bear much fruit.

We too experience this whenever we stand under the holy cross of Christ, in the place of bloody death which has borne the most precious fruits for the sustaining of man in this life and in the life hereafter.

What are the fruits of the death of Jesus?

If I had the opportunity I would talk privately with each member of this large assembly and I would ask each one how he has experienced throughout his Christian life the fruit of the death of Christ. I believe I would receive as many different answers to my question as there are people gathered here. Each reply would testify that Jesus—the grain of wheat sown by God— has brought forth fruit without limit.

5

Our world assembly points to two of these innumerable fruits —two extremely important ones, namely, that our freedom and our unity are rooted in the death of Christ.

All of us who have come here with grateful hearts from all corners of the world are reminded of our precious freedom and unity. In this life we already have the first fruits of this freedom and unity. In the life eternal we shall experience them in their fullness.

One of the fruits of the death of Christ is this: Christ frees.

From what?

From the words of Jesus I conclude first of all that He frees me from myself, from my narrow selfishness. "He who loves his life loses it, and he who hates his life in this world will keep it for eternal life."

And this is a blessed freedom, that we need not constantly live in the bondage of human selfishness.

You all know the words which were spoken by the great teacher of our Church, Martin Luther: ". . . who has redeemed me, a lost and condemned creature, purchased and won me from all sin, from death, and from the power of the devil. . . ."

Are these dry statements?

Only insofar as we regard them as a lesson to be memorized.

But if someone, by the power of Christ, has been able to break with his besetting sin, if someone in confronting death has been able to avoid freezing with fear, and has been given strength to face it with triumphant anticipation, if someone has felt in his heart the power of faith which has enabled him to break Satan's chains, then upon the lips of this man the words of Luther are not dry, lifeless statements, but are rather notes of jubilation.

And for what does Jesus free us?

To this question Jesus gives an answer, too: "If any one serves me, he must follow me; and where I am: there shall my servant be also; if any one serves me, the Father will honor him."

And we all know Luther's reply: ". . . in order that I might be his own, live under him in his kingdom, and serve him. . . ."

This is what Jesus wants.

Yes, my friends! I can imagine what you are thinking. "From one bondage to another! Is this the freedom of the Christian man?"

You have probably heard many sermons about the man who bought a slave, and when he had paid the price, set him free. This story may be a primitive analogy. But it faithfully expresses the basic meaning and true happiness of the Christian life. Our life contains no greater happiness than to be set free from sin, the fear of death, and the torment of damnation, and then, with the joy of complete liberation, to turn to Christ and to serve Him.

The other fruit of the death of Christ is that it unites.

It unites us with Him: "If any one serves me, he must follow me; and where I am, there shall my servant be also."

It unites us with God: "If any one serves me, the Father will honor him."

And after His resurrection His Holy Spirit has continually been calling and gathering all those who believe in Him.

This He did with all of us when He gave us His precious message of salvation, when He received us as His own in Baptism and when He unites us in the Holy Supper. This He does, according to our faith, even now as He gathers us in this great assembly.

I want to ask you all to give thanks to Jesus for His gift of unity which He has bestowed upon us through faith in Him so that, though we may never have met before, though we may be living under entirely different earthly circumstances, we are nevertheless friends and brothers as members of one body, the universal Church of Christ. And I trust that, driven and encouraged by this awareness, we shall leave this assembly committed

7

to the task of preserving and increasing this unity, so that we may at all times dwell with our Lord.

I must once again return to the beginning of our text. We have read that those Greeks had turned to Philip and Andrew with their request: "We wish to see Jesus." And we have seen that Philip and Andrew fulfilled this request. But we are the Philips and Andrews of today. Let us rejoice with all our hearts in our discipleship. Let us rejoice in our closeness to Christ. But let us reveal Him to those who are yearning for Him, and even to those who are hostile toward Him. To the world enslaved by sin our lives must be witnesses to the Christ who frees. To the world divided and factious let us show Christ who truly unites.

You have heard these words from an aging disciple of Christ. This disciple would now in concluding his formal message give a personal testimony to his Lord and Savior. He would like to say how many times in his life he has experienced the forgiving grace of Jesus Christ. And he would also like to say that when he was in bondage in the most literal sense of the word, Christ gave him royal freedom. And what a joy it was to be able to experience this freedom!

And he would like to say how sweet were the fruits of Christian unity in his life, especially in times when the world offered to him only bitterness.

I am now looking over this large assembly. I see all those who have rendered so many good and loyal services to their Church. And I am also glad to see the many young representatives of our world-wide Lutheran Church—those who carry the future in their hands. I am speaking to all of you. Our world assembly is now looking to Christ, who does have the power to free and to unite us. I merely want to underscore this central theme of our gathering as, looking back upon a lifetime of experience, I say to you:

Christ alone can set us free!

Christ alone can unite us!

He said: "The hour has come for the Son of man to be glorified."

Brethren! May this world assembly serve the glory of the Son of man, Jesus Christ! Amen.

Bishop Hanns Lilje

As head of the Lutheran World Federation (1952-57), Bishop Lilje leads the cooperative activities of 57 member Churches in 29 countries, representing nearly 50 million of the 70 million Lutherans in the world.

Born in 1899 in Hannover, Germany, he was educated at the Universities of Leipzig and Goettingen and the Cloister Loccum Seminary at Hannover. He was general secretary of the German Student Christian Movement and vice president of the World Student Christian Federation (1927-35). He served as general secretary of the Lutheran World Convention, forerunner of the LWF (1937-46).

An outspoken anti-Nazi, he was imprisoned by the Gestapo in 1944, sentenced to death by a special tribunal in January of 1945 and liberated by U.S. troops in May of 1945.

He was named Bishop of the Lutheran Church of Hannover in 1947. He was elected president of the United Evangelical Lutheran Church of Germany in 1955. He is also a member of policy-making Central Committee of the World Council of Churches.

Christ Frees
and Unites

THIS great assembly of Lutheran Christians from all the world for which the prayers and sacrifices of so many churches in the entire world have prepared, is faced with one task, and it is a task which requires an act of spiritual courage. We are at the point of expressing a confession of our faith. It, like any real confession, must be made in the presence of God and before the eyes of the world.

As we set out to do this, we are bound to consider a great historical parallel. At the outset of our common task, it will be well to remember those large assemblies of the early church, the ecumenical councils. That these councils exert an influence down to the present time is due to the fact that they accomplished the clarification of spiritual issues in a concise form. The symbols, in which they summarized the dogmatic thinking of their time and which they passed on to others as well-defined judgments, were secured in the fervent spiritual struggle with the contemporary world. They have preserved their vitality down to the present day because they are the result of genuine and essential controversy.

We must not desire to do less. As so many representatives

from her congregations in all the world meet together, the Lutheran Church today must, to be sure, keep clearly in mind the message which has been entrusted to her by her forefathers. But she dare not make her confession by simply repeating the thoughts and words of the past. On the contrary, whatever she has to confess she must say to the world in which we live *today*. For the moment in which we set forth our confession of the living God is the present moment, the immediate world in whose fascinating spectrum of longing and dread, technical triumphs and world-wide catastrophes we have been placed.

We must face this world realistically. There can be no doubt that its most conspicuous characteristic is dread (Angst). Our world, rent asunder by countless, almost insuperable tensions, is nowhere so united as here. The memory of the tragedies which have filled the first half of this fateful century hovers over mankind like a torturing, everpresent shadow. Racial and religious, political and economic differences disappear wherever there arise the dark clouds of fear, the dread of a new war, the horror of a catastrophe the consequences of which would be beyond reckoning. There is in our world today an Internationale of dread which embraces more men than do any of the great political ideologies.

Secondly, we must consider the great transformations wrought by modern technology. This has altered our present world more vitally and more lastingly than has ever been done before in the previous eras of human history. This technical development, which before our very eyes moves toward perfection and which basically recognizes almost no insoluble problems, has brought the nations closer to one another than any other previous force in history. An Internationale of technological civilization has arisen from which no part of the world is exempted. There is an intimate relationship between this technological revolution which has drawn all nations into its vortex and the union of fear in which we live today. In Central Africa and Europe, in Japan and Alaska, these advances in civilization have surely created the same general conditions for life; the possibilities for travel, for communication, for hygienic living conditions are almost the same anywhere in the world. Nevertheless, they have brought mankind no closer to happiness. Even the most serious social tensions and the racial uprisings pale to insignificance alongside the fact that among these thousands of new technological possibilities, a single one overshadows all others—namely, the possibility of universal annihilation. Thus does man learn, even though he may not know it, the truth of the Biblical statement: "For what will it profit a man if he gains the whole world and forfeits his life?" (Matt. 16:26.) Even the communistic countries which still hold to a naive belief in inevitable progress, and in the unlimited power and goodness of man, have demonstrated in their political utterances that the fear of these weapons of annihilation is beginning to undermine their ideological security.

A deep-seated intellectual and spiritual insecurity is the third characteristic of the world in which we live. On the one hand, it is related to a natural and understandable event. Our entire scientific view of the world has been drastically changed because of the research of nuclear physicists; through their study of physical aspects, they have been led forward to new and profound philosophical insights. Scarcely a single fundamental concept of the world view held hitherto has remained unchanged; not even the apparently axiomatic concept of casuality has been able to maintain itself in the face of this revolutionary process. Every philosophy from which the spiritual life of our western civilization derives nourishment has been affected by this revolution. The result is a sense of insecurity which asserts itself everywhere.

Wide areas of the world are today experiencing a major crisis in their faiths; the so-called Christian lands and nations are touched by this no less than the rest of the world. It ought not to be said, however, that our generation is irreligious; to the contrary—it is permeated by notable religious tendencies. The classic, old, non-Christian religions are witnessing something like a renaissance; it is not our task to determine how much of this is a genuine renewal and how much is only external activity or sterile restoration. The philosophical movements of our day are inquiring into the most important matter of our generation—man. But it is impossible to inquire about man without coming to grips with the question of God. All of these religious and pseudo-religious movements, however, are characterized far more by the feeling of longing than by certainty. The real philosophical and religious dilemma of our time lies in the fact that man does not want any religious illusions and he has no power to believe. It is honest renunciation. Disregarding certain currents of dialectical materialism which certainly is not characteristic of modern thought, there is no anti-Christian trend of thought in our generation worthy of mention; yet there is no universal movement which can revitalize Christianity, either. We are living in a nihilistic world.

This is the dark background of the world against which our Assembly as a member of the Christian Church shall confess its faith. In the face of such a world situation as exists at this time, the repetition of past creeds and past judgments will not suffice. The very will not to be satisfied with antiquated or even reworked statements has compelled us to set as the theme of this Assembly: Christ frees and unites.

We desire to make our confession here and now.

For this basic reason, we desire for ourselves two special gifts of the Holy Spirit: in the first place, a clear and dynamic mind with which we may set forth as clearly as possible this great message which of course is not only given to our church; and secondly, profound, moral courage so that we can witness in the world in which we live to the insights of our faith without fear

14

and doubt, without indifference and false self-confidence. Illuminatio and disciplina, fides and fortitudo—let these be the gifts of the Holy Spirit for which we pray in these days.

I

Our theme begins with the strongest and boldest of confessions: Christ. The meaning of this confession is not that we confess Christ in addition to other statements, but rather that in this confused and distressed world, we acknowledge no other guide but Him, the Son of God and the Son of man. Transcending our world, pursued as it is by fear and uncertainty, is the silent majesty of our crucified and risen Lord. The most important act of our present confession is that we direct our eyes toward Him. Like an electric current, there ought to go out from this great international assembly a great, united stimulus of faith as we renew our pledge of allegiance to Him. We do not seek to escape from the world by retiring into the cells of piety when we assert this; rather, we seek to orient ourselves toward Christ who is the answer to all the difficulties, anxieties and fears of our generation.

Here we must make it clear whether our faith can be related to the present, whether Christ really can be the answer to our present distress. To take the most important and at the same time most simple example by way of illustration, nothing so binds all of mankind together at this moment as does fear. Since Einstein's famous letter in which he expresses profound concern about atomic weapons, the fear of the possibilities for such a war has spread over the globe like a deluge. Scholars and statesmen are agreed that here mankind must act together. Neither a workable control of atomic weapons nor their complete renunciation (which would be even better) is feasible unless there is a general willingness among the nations to co-operate. But why do we think so little of the chances for such co-operation? Is it not because we consider mankind incapable of so much common moral strength? This is a grave and dangerous state of affairs, compelling us to stop and think. If this indispensable willingness is to grow, a completely new attitude is required among human beings. We Christians must never grow tired of proclaiming that the only one from whom such a total renewal of man can proceed is Jesus Christ, who, by His resurrection, has deprived death of its power and has brought a new way of life into the world.

This then is what we mean when we pledge allegiance to the Lord in the very first word of our theme. We do not mean that He is merely Lord for the Church and certainly not that He is a kind of benevolent patron of the Lutheran Church (although that is included), but we mean that He is Lord for the world— the world in which we live, the world which needs a Savior from its anxiety and its fear of death.

Only in this way can we be a Lutheran Church. With a deep sense of gratitude do we recall that our reformer never thought of establishing a separate church. He is distinguished from the founders of many modern sects and religions by the fact that he declined as a matter of principle the plan for founding a new church, desiring only the return to the one true Church of the New Testament. Related to this is the fact that his only theological and canonical standard was Gloria Christi. It is illuminating to note the decisive meaning which this formula had for Luther. Today also, it is the only valid standard. If the Lutheran Church wishes to find her way through the uncertainties of faith and through the threat to the existence of present day man, she must not ask, What is Lutheran? but rather, What is consonant with Christ?

For this fundamental reason, the Lutheran Church *can* never appear as the champion of historic confessionalism. To be sure, she has reason to be thankful for her history because Christen-

16

dom was richly blessed by the dawn of the Reformation and because the beginning of the church was remarkably free of the curse of ambition, power and force. She is also aware and grateful for that chain which unites her with her past, the great successio fidelium, the spiritual succession of believers and confessors; among these, she numbers the church fathers of our Lutheran Church, Bach and Paul Gerhardt, Harms and Loehe, Muhlenberg and Soederblom and many more. But the essence of her faith is that she acknowledges here and now that Jesus Christ is her only Lord. The initial point at which we are united to that chain of believers is not Luther, but Christ. Hence her task is not the preservation of an historical heritage, but it is the confession here and now of the substance of this heritage: Jesus Christ Himself. She is truly the Lutheran Church when she confesses her allegiance to Jesus Christ, not when she refers back to Martin Luther.

In this day and age, it is no simple task to proclaim our allegiance to Jesus Christ. If the Lutheran Church sincerely wishes to witness to Christ in the very present, a large measure of strict spiritual clarification will be demanded from her. Just as high a degree of the inner assurance of faith is required if, among all of the enticements of realization, the Church of the Reformation wishes to neglect nothing that is really essential. And finally she must be aware that the Christian witness can be proclaimed in the world not only by intelligence and theology, but above all by the humble obedience of the sanctified; this is still the surest, most trustworthy and hence the most effective means of witnessing to Christ in the world today.

Thus we are to understand the total theme of our Plenary Assembly: it is the attempt to confess here and now, within this world perplexed by a multitude of questions and anxieties, our faith in the Lord Jesus Christ—the only one from whom we expect help.

We do this in the presence of a world whose secret expectation we know is as great as its scepticism. No Christian can speak of his Lord today without taking cognizance of the heavy burden of a century-old scepticism. What we call the modern mind is indeed extremely complex and certainly is not clearly definable; but many who refer to this concept mean thereby that it no longer seems possible to believe the forms of traditional Christianity and the organized churches. This is not an embarrassment peculiar to the Lutheran Church, but she must face up to it in a special way. For a Church which for the sake of the truth of Christ and for the freedom of the human conscience once separated itself from the aged body of Christendom must be receptive, in a special sense, to the scepticism of modern man and to his doubts concerning matters of belief. Provided that we understand it correctly, the Lutheran Church in her essential form is the most modern because faith can exist within her only when it is grounded upon ultimate truthfulness. Then she ought to be able most directly to meet modern man in the place where he is most sincere.

Thus in the face of all these problems which are presented by the sceptical attitude of modern man, we confess our allegiance to Christ. In so doing, we are open not only to the critical questions which are raised by science, philosophy and technology; but in addition, we are aware of everything that determines the modern attitude toward life. Even though modern man is afflicted by spiritual uncertainties brought upon him by the progress of scientific thought, talking with him is not without promise. We know from the testimony of several of the greatest natural scientists of our generation that no exclusive contradiction needs to exist between natural science and faith in God. Even the doubts with respect to the historical reliability of the New Testament reports which were raised at the turn of the century appear to us today in a different light; even such a critical-scientific exegete as Bultmann can say that the doubts concerning the historical existence of Jesus deserve no refutation. But this attitude towards life which is held by modern man does not generally take into account the controversies of scientific theologians and does not readily yield to persuasion. For what can the witness of the Christian accomplish if it meets a spiritual attitude where the great religious and philosophical statements are generally doubted? For when man has come to distrust statements of faith, it makes little difference whether he is summoned to faith in the name of some church or under the auspices of some philosophy. Only one who has understood and respected his sceptical questions will gain his attention; and naturally, he will take notice if he meets a clear, definitive and creditable expression of faith. In such a situation, it is mandatory that his scepticism be met not by a fearful, minimal apologetic, but rather by the power and clarity of faith.

The late Dr. Elert, one of the great teachers of the Lutheran Church, once said that, in the early church only that which was liturgically acceptable was dogmatically acceptable. This means that no doctrinal statement has validity for the church unless it is possible for it to simultaneously fit into the framework of the hymn of praise. If she is rightly to fulfill her task, the confessing and teaching church must always be the praising and adoring church.

In this sense, and in no other, do we develop the common witness of this great Assembly: Christ frees and unites.

II

Boldly the total theme strikes at the heart of the present-day problem that concerns us all with the declaration that Christ frees; and that means, to be sure, that He is the only, the most important and the most effective liberator. Our theme links the center of our faith with the problems of our time. From the personal insight and decision of faith on the part of the individual, there is a line which leads directly through the decisive points in the world's present turbulent condition to the throne of God. Only when this line is real and not just imagined can the claim of our faith be justified that it is not merely a theory, but a reality. That is a bold assertion. Interpretation of the world based upon justification? If it is really true that the central doctrine of the Reformation, JUSTIFICATIO IMPII, contains the key to the understanding of the present-day condition of our world, then two things are immediately apparent: (1) the doctrine of justification cannot suffice as the central interpretation of the gospel if it does not hold good in the kind of world in which we live. (2) No attempt to interpret the condition of the present-day world can be adequate if it does not lead to this profound insight of our faith. Both of these are intimately related. We must guard against the misunderstanding, however, that the complete insight of our faith resulted from some kind of interpretation of present-day events. The given condition of the world cannot provide the source of Christian perception because it can be understood only from itself. The only source of Christian insight is, and will remain, the living God who reveals and manifests Himself ubi et quando visum est Eo—where and when He so desires.

The question as to the concrete historical meaning of this theme remains to be considered. The theme of freedom has special significance for the Western World. The history of Europe and America has taken place under the banner of freedom, and today as it passes through a crisis of the first order, it is concerned primarily with the question whether it can still derive its historical mission from the idea of freedom.

Now there can be no doubt that the idea of freedom in the Western World is a legacy from Christianity. For freedom is not only something in the political sphere (ancient Greece, which again and again is erroneously regarded as a source of European thinking as regards freedom, was at best and in its historically most productive periods, i.e., under Pericles, nothing less than a brilliant, genial, but totalitarian dictatorship). *Man* is undoubtedly the real basis of freedom. In the Western ideas of freedom, the question is not primarily that of a political program, but rather concerns man's independence in his historical and personal destiny.

If the history of the Western world is correctly understood, it is seen to be concerned with this ultimate self-assertion of man. This theme explains its greatness as well as its errors. If it is at this point that the Western man has lost the understanding of his existence, then this is the only point where he can regain it.

At this point our theme reaches beyond the rather narrow historical sweep of the West. For the question of man's destiny, his existence in this world, is a universal theme. Hence the answer of the Church of the Reformation is of more than mere denominational significance.

Our theme would be justified even if these world-wide perspectives did not exist. The question of man is always at the same time the question of his relationship to God. That the Lutheran Church has never accepted as valid an answer to the question of man's destiny which did not include at the same time his ultimate status as a creature before God has always been her greatness as a Church. At the same time, it has been the peculiarity of the Lutheran proclamation of the gospel that, in the light of church history, she has carried out this message in its most radical form. This distinguishing mark is especially apparent in the Lutheran concept of man. This radicalness consists of the fact that she asserts that man in the presence of God can be regarded only as the absolutely and completely guilty one, the godless one. The historical failure as well as the importance of the Lutheran Church can be seen in this fact, that she has always

21

proclaimed this assertion. For modern man has understandably turned away from the radical nature of this assertion and has ardently defended man's natural goodness. Similarly, the Roman Church, as everyone knows, has shied away from the radicalness of this assertion and has sought to mitigate it by other, more plausible, anthropological theories. In view of present-day philosophy, however, this radical view of man reveals its validity. Les extremes se touchent (the extremes touch one another)—at this point the understanding of man by Existentialism, this view of man without illusion and without pathos, meets the anthropology of the Reformation with its insight that man cannot answer God once in a thousand times (Job 9:3). Man is remote from God; he is godless, impious.

Although externally, the Lutheran anthropology resembles the pessimistic interpretation of man as Existentialism presents it, the decisive difference is, after all, unmistakable. The Reformation proclaimed that God Himself has taken in hand these hopeless conditions. He does not leave man in the state of absolute godlessness. Though man can be nothing else but a sinner, God accepts him as though he were not a sinner, but His own child. He does it in the form of a majestic proclamation. He erases all of the demands required by justice in a magnificent act of acquittal. He declares him to be guiltless and just and so treats him. This He does through Jesus Christ. We need not repeat the many ingenious theories of Lutheran scholasticism, namely those of the 16th and 17th century orthodoxy, although they do bear luminous testimony to the scholarly seriousness of our predecessors. For the moment we need only to be clear on this one point: the Lutheran doctrine of justification through faith is the most sublime, the most profound and the most radical foundation for the true freedom of man. If this is true, the Lutheran Church must state clearly that Christ makes us free and she must state the manner in which He accomplishes this.

22

This she must do in a twofold manner—with respect to the individual, and with respect to the community in which we live.

If the fundamental significance of this basic insight of the Reformation as it applies to the understanding of *human existence* is to be correctly described, one must call attention both to the radical nature of this thought and to its decisive paradox.

The radicalness of this thought is that it destroys and renders impossible all attempts by man to "justify" himself, i.e., to escape by aid of heroic anthropologies from the final, realistic evaluation of himself. For it is not said that man is bad but it is asserted that he can in no wise satisfy the ultimate ethical and personal standard, namely the judgment of God.

The paradox of this thought consists in the knowledge that just this type of self-evaluation of man without illusions can open up the way out of his dilemma. All attempts to help himself plunge him only deeper into difficulty and distress, and those who wish to help him in this human way do the same. The message of salvation is that God does what man cannot do; that in Jesus Christ, He has demolished the prison within which man has become enclosed. The simile of prison from which man is set free is not strong enough for the Biblical proclamation; it states that man has passed from death to life. Much is said and written today concerning the observation that modern man has lost the capacity of understanding these symbols of the Christian message. Quite likely that is right, and if so, this is an occasion for Christendom to engage in humble self-examination. But though the capacity for understanding these symbols has been lost today, the ability to understand the substance to which they refer has certainly not been lost. And it is here that the distress and the hope of contemporary man lie very close together. For once he sees through the heroic illusions, his faith in the provisional authorities of the world is most seriously shaken. Yet he has not thereby been freed from the basic danger of losing his freedom again to other human authorities on another day. Only when, through the creative act of the mercy of God, he is tied to the real, final and highest authority in the world, to God Himself, does he gain at the same time freedom from subservience to all tentative, transitory human authorities.

This does not imply that henceforth he ought to live by disregarding all human authority. But he will accord them obedience in freedom, and he will honor them as human authorities whose ultimate criteria are derived from divine authority. This is also the way in which he can find again real human fellowship. Human society today is severely threatened in all its forms —in the intimate circle of the family and of marriage, and in the relationship of the older generation with the younger; in the social order of a nation and in the international community of nations. One of the most important diagnostic insights of Christianity is the observation that true fellowship in the internal life of a nation and in the relations between nations can exist only in freedom; and, further, that this freedom can be attained only from the innermost center of the personality, namely, faith.

III

Thus there follows the continuation of this thematic statement: Christ frees and *unites*.

A witness to the *world* is the first thing that is herein contained. The threat to human society in all its forms has reached the point of destruction. It is a strange process: while the means of communication approach ever greater perfection, so in like degree does the capacity for social intercourse decline. The most uncanny aspect is that the power for the development of social intercourse simply collapses from within. This deficient faculty for individual contact is a growing danger which threatens personal life. Related to this is the fact that there exists so little capacity among the nations, the races and the social groups for self-evident, natural interchange of ideas. What makes the con-

24

temporary world order so threatening is the lack of the ability to solve the historical and political problems of the world by a common effort. The fruitless nature of the many attempts to attack the decisive problems of the present world is related to the fact that this fundamental incapability of living together harmoniously often is not even recognized.

This absence of real fellowship cannot be overcome solely by organizational efforts; it requires a healing brought about by faith. This is the witness which Christianity at all costs must emphasize. It is by no means sufficient that she concern herself with socio-political matters and attack individual problems of a social nature. Regardless of how essential all that she can do in this direction may be, her decisive task must be to direct attention to that point at which alone human fellowship can be renewed. One of the most serious and practical problems confronting the Lutheran Church is whether she can state in a credible manner that only a person who lives by the longsuffering and mercy of God can associate with his fellow men in patience and friendliness. The strongest source of lasting harmony among human beings is the experience of forgiveness. In this sense, the only valid and helpful starting point for the improvement of community life is the justification of the sinner, of the godless. The task of the Lutheran Church is to show clearly that all secondary measures aimed at restoring fellowship among the nations will remain fruitless efforts if the decisive prerequisite of justifying mercy is not present.

The witness of the Church at this point will remain ineffective unless the will toward fellowship among the *churches* themselves gains new force. The witness that it is only Christ who unites is the most important contribution made by the Lutheran Church to the Ecumenical Movement. Since the churches in their more recent development have moved toward one another through the Ecumenical Movement, a danger exists that they will seek unity along lines which cannot carry them completely to the goal but will finally falter after some initially practical and useful ecclesiastical impulses. At the same time there is the danger that organizational demands which are either completely impractical or are impossible of attainment will transform the ecumenical mission of Christianity into nomism which enervates man because he never completely reaches his goal.

By way of contrast, the witness that it is Christ alone who unites, emphasizes the fact that the unity of Christianity *is already present* in Christ. Hence it is reasonable to be concerned about the union of churches because in Christ this union already exists. Credo unam sanctam ecclesiam catholicam—that means that this one holy, Christian Church does exist, not that it must be created by means of organization. It exists beyond all organizational, ecclesiastical, even dogmatic efforts, because Christ is the one Lord of Christendom, because a church can exist only where He is present, and because the Church can exist only when she confirms the presence of her Lord in faith and obedience. By testifying to this existing union of the Church, the Lutheran Church points to the center and the source of all ecumenical movements. If this focal point is lost or displaced, then immediately all lines are distorted. If this source is no longer known or regarded, then the Ecumenical Movement is condemned to an impotent routine. Christ alone unites. Hence an emphatic yes in favor of the Ecumenical Movement, but nevertheless a yes which is irrevocably committed to Him and to Him alone.

Ignatius of Antioch (in his epistle to the Romans, 3:3) has said, "Christianity is not a matter of argumentation but of true greatness." This ardent Christian, who was called upon to confirm his faith in the time of persecution, has characterized with this sentence the attitude in which the Christian must render his witness in the world even today. It is not by reason of argumentation, by intellectual and historical analysis or other secular sophistries that the Church is effective, but in every question she is effective solely by virtue of the firmness and clarity of her confession. May the Church receive as a gift from her Lord the strength for this challenge! May also our Assembly be filled with that power which is more than argument, namely the expression of that joyousness ascribed to the first messengers of Christ.

Dr. Chitose Kishi

Dr. Kishi was elected president of the Japan Evangelical Lutheran Church in 1956 and also heads up its Theological Seminary. His headquarters are in Tokyo.

Born in 1898, he visited the U.S. as an exchange student and received his B.A. degree from Roanoke College, Va., in 1923. He also attended the University of South Carolina, Southern Lutheran Theological Seminary at Columbia, S. C., Hartford (Conn.) Seminary and the University of Leipzig, East Germany.

On his return to Japan, he was ordained in 1928 and held pastorates in Kurume, Moji, East Kobe and Kyota. He was imprisoned by the government during the war on charges of "preaching for peace." An author, he has also translated books from Swedish and English into Japanese. He received an honorary D.D. from Lenoir Rhyne College at Hickory, N. C., in 1953.

The Freedom
We Have in Christ

I

THE twentieth century has already passed through turbulent times, having experienced two great world wars. Their aftermath presents many complicated problems which still await solution. The solutions to which men resort reflect some characteristic feature of this century. From one point of view, the twentieth century may be characterized by Revolution and Reconciliation. In the former, we see the awakening of nationalism in Asia and Africa; the revolutionary upheaval of the proletariat; and the revolt of the oppressed against totalitarian communistic regimes. These are attended by the resurgence of religions such as Buddhism, Hinduism and Mohammedanism, and the growing use of Atomic energy. In Reconciliation, we see the world wide missionary enterprise, seeking to unite all nations through the proclamation of redemption accomplished by Jesus Christ. Both these are concerned with freedom of humanity.

In regard to the freedom based on human efforts we may observe a strange phenomena; namely, it would appear that

29

when an individual or a nation gains a much desired freedom in one area, they are immediately enslaved in another. In social life, youth in revolt increasingly discards Christian faith and practice, giving itself to wantonness. The result is therefore not freedom, but rather enslavement to lust. We sense here the singular fact that in human effort even for freedom there seems to be some sort of judgment upon it. The tide of nationalism is rising high in every country in the world, particularly in Asia and Africa. There is good reason for it, because there are few who do not love their own country. But as extreme and demonic nationalism asserts itself, very often it brings about a consequence contrary to its expectation. This was the case with Japanese militarism. Human efforts are self-defeating and even self-destroying. What has been called the "demonic" is evident. That is to say, the power which freedom seemingly has in and over itself is grasped by another power which sets at naught all its attempts to realize itself and frustrates all its good intentions. Autonomy is constantly transformed into heteronomy. This singular fact has led to the disruption, conflict, self-destruction, meaninglessness and despair in all realms of life. For many it means the loss of an ultimate meaning in life. Consequently there is a reluctant—on the part of some; a cynical—on the part of others; a fanatical—on the part of still others—surrender to powers, the nature of which nobody can fully grasp or control. This is a notable phase of our human predicament.

Let us see this situation for a moment in the light of Revolution and Reconciliation. Revolution is the human effort to gain freedom by overthrowing the yoke of bondage, whereas Reconciliation is the expression of freedom given by God through Jesus Christ. But when we examine them more closely in the light of God's redemptive activity, we will find that Revolution may not be antagonistic to Reconciliation. Through Revolution the yoke of the old is thrown off, but through Reconciliation the yoke of the new is prepared and given. God has given us the law and the Gospel. The law shows us the human contradiction and prepares the way for Revolution. But freedom is not realized by Revolution alone. Rather it is reconciliation that is the revolutionary power. "The Lord kills and brings to life; he brings down to Sheol and raises up. The Lord makes poor and makes rich; he brings low, he also exalts. He raises up the poor from dust; he lifts the needy from the ash heap, to make them sit with princes and inherit a seat of honor" (I Sam. 2: 6-8a).

Why then does God do this? Let us hear what the Lord said to Jeremiah:

"Behold, I have put my words in your mouth. See, I have set you this day over nations and over kingdoms, to pluck and to break down, to destroy and to overthrow, to build and to plant" (Jer. 1:9-10).

Through this passage we learn that the Lord stands over nations and kingdoms, using Jeremiah as His agency. He is responsible for all nations and kingdoms, and has the sovereignty over the world. The Scriptures testify that the triune God is the creator and preserver of all things, visible and invisible. God's sovereignty extends to every area of man's existence. In every moment God confronts man with His sovereign authority. Here we find an answer to our question.

The sovereignty of God was fully revealed when the lordship of Christ was made known in the fullness of time. The lordship of Christ and the manner in which it was manifested is beyond human understanding. Thus the freedom which is born of such a lordship is quite different from the freedom based on human efforts.

31

Here we are led to consider "the freedom we have in Christ." The emphasis does not fall on "the freedom we have" but on "Christ." When "Christ" enters the realm of freedom, its meaning is entirely changed. The pivotal point is Christ. Christ makes any freedom gained by human efforts problematical. This does not imply, however, that He ignores the freedom sought by individuals or nations, nor that He passes by the unspeakable misery of people oppressed by various forms of tyrannic powers. On the contrary, He is more concerned about the freedom of mankind than any human being on earth. His whole life was devoted to the complete and perfect deliverance of self-centered humanity.

According to the Scriptures, the way in which Christ delivered humanity is quite extraordinary. It is revolutionary and at the same time reconciliatory. Christ identified Himself with humanity and yet retained His divine nature. By His coming under the law He obeyed and fulfilled the law to the extent that He was crucified on the Cross. Because of His death, "God has highly exalted Him and bestowed on Him the name which is above every name, that at the name of Jesus every knee should bow in heaven and on earth and under the earth and every tongue confess that Jesus Christ is Lord, to the glory of God, the Father" (Phil. 2:9-11). Two things, death and resurrection, which contradict each other are united in one Person, Jesus Christ. It is legitimate to say that the Lordship of Christ was realized through the Cross on Calvary, and He has delivered mankind through it.

Christ as such is active and aggressive under all circumstances, and is the Lord even over the realm of Satan. He is victorious even in apparent defeat. This is the divine logic demonstrated once for all before the eyes of the world in the Cross of Christ. For this reason Paul says, "Thanks be to God, that you who were once slaves of sin have become obedient from the heart to the standard of teaching to which you were committed, and having

been set free from sin, have become slaves of righteousness"
(Rom. 6:17-22). Freedom in Christ means man's removal from
the Satanic realm to the promised kingdom of eternal life.

II

To disabuse man of the illusory forms of freedom which are
the object of his efforts, man must know his own reality. Man's
reality as revealed through the Cross of Christ is miserable and
utterly hopeless. In Augsburg Confession Art. II it is stated that
"since the fall of Adam, all men begotten in the natural way are
born with sin, that is, without the fear of God, without trust in
God, and with concupiscence and that this disease, or vice of
origin, is truly sin, even now condemning and bringing eternal
death upon those not born again through Baptism and the Holy
Ghost." Man born without the fear of God or without trust in
God, is spiritually blind, deprived of even an awareness of God.
He is sick unto death. What freedom he has is that of a blind
man. His freedom resembles the freedom of a falling stone. It
has only one direction, that is, the way which leads to further
separation from God and deeper sin. There is consequently no
fellowship between God and man, namely, there is no true
dialogue. There is only monologue which inevitably leads to
pride and despair. Men who have pride before God are those
who "have forsaken the Lord." "They have despised the Holy
One of Israel, they are utterly estranged" (Isaiah 1:4). The condition of such people is that "the whole heart is sick, and the
whole heart faint." This human situation may be designated as
egocentric, and is manifested in all spheres of human life. It is
true that "none is righteous, no not one; no one understands, no
one seeks for God. All have turned aside, together they have gone
wrong; no one does good, not even one" (Rom. 3:10-12).

Many forms of self-centered religion originate from the matrix
of egocentricity. In such egocentric and self-seeking religions

emphasis is laid on man's activity. Every thing is planned to satisfy an extremely selfish desire. However spiritualized it may be, man is still the center and God is merely a profit producing agency used to fulfill man's unsatiable desire.

When we turn our attention to Christianity, we see there an entirely different situation. There a person who is at once divine and human meets us; He meets us to become the mediator between God and us as sinners. According to the Scriptures, He is at once Prophet, Priest and King. Let us mark each of these.

A prophet has a close relation to the life of people, as in the case of the Old Testament prophets. What they speak is the will of God, applied to all human affairs such as the politico-economic affairs of the nation, or relations with other nations. However, their words are not their own but God's. Jesus, on the other hand, speaks, prophesies and promises. He speaks His own words with authority. The range of His interests includes everything, extending from the least to the greatest. Nothing escapes His eyes. Even the things that will occur in the future are crystal clear to Him. He foretold the catastrophic destruction of Jerusalem. He warned Peter of his denial. But He tells a more astounding thing to us, saying, "the hour is coming, and now is, when the dead will hear the voice of the Son of God, and those who hear will live" (John 5:25). Christ does this that we may marvel! What He says is the prophecy that He brings about an entirely new situation which the old world has never seen. Again He said "that there would be a catastrophic shaking of the foundation of the universe and the Son of man would be seen coming on the cloud of heaven with power and great glory." All what He says are not empty words of an abnormal day-dreamer but are seriously concerned with the salvation of man. Really He is God's final word to man. Christ as Prophet has shattered wisdom of this world at its very foundation.

Secondly, Jesus Christ as priest is also incomparable. The

priesthood in the Old Testament was temporal for as Hebrews (Heb. 7:23) states the priests "were many in number because they were prevented by death from continuing in office." Furthermore, they had to prepare the sacrifice for themselves and for the people they represented. But in case of Jesus, He himself is the sacrifice, and at the same time the priest who offers it. God "made Him to be sin who knew no sin" for our sake. He is "the lamb that takes away the sin of the world." At the same time "when Christ appeared as a high priest of good things that have come, then through the greater and more perfect tent (not made with hands, that is, not of this creation) he entered once for all into the Holy Place taking not the blood of goats and calves but his own blood, thus securing an eternal redemption" (Heb. 9:11-12). In the Old Testament, redemption was secured by the annual sacrifice by the priests. This was a shadow of that which was to come.

In the fullness of time Jesus came and demonstrated the full meaning of the sacrifice which alone pleases God. The sacrifice and its officiating priests are one and the same person, the truth of which is inconceivable to human logic. Through such an extraordinary way the idea of the sacrifice has been completely changed. St. Paul says, "O the depth of the riches and wisdom and knowledge of God! How unsearchable are his judgments and how inscrutable his ways!" (Rom. 11:33.) And this high priest is able to sympathize with our weakness and "in every respect has been tempted as we are, yet without sinning" (Heb. 4:15). He went into the depth of human suffering as He shed tears over Lazarus' death. Nothing can take place of Him as a sacrifice and no one can replace Him as a priest.

Thirdly, the kingship of Christ is repeated again and again in the Scriptures. There is "one Lord, Jesus Christ, through whom all things and through whom we exist" (I Cor. 8:5-6). He is also called "Wonderful Counselor, Mighty God, Everlasting

Father, Prince of Peace" (Isaiah 9:6). He is Immanuel, God incarnate. Meekness and lowliness characterized His life on earth. Yet He could have commanded more than twelve legions of angels against His enemy if He had so desired (Matt. 26:53). Although He said that His kingdom is not of this world, this does not imply that He has nothing to do with this world. As God incarnate He lived and walked among men. His activity was at once revolutionary and reconciliatory. Namely He broke down "the dividing wall of hostility, by abolishing in His flesh the law of commandments and ordinances that He might create in Himself one new man in place of two, so making peace, and might reconcile us both to God in one body through the cross thereby bringing the hostility to an end" (Eph. 2:15-16). He served all but "has put all things under His feet" (Eph. 1:22). As King, Christ is both lowly and regal. He is simultaneously destroyer and creator, the suffering servant and Lord of Lords. Thus the conception of lordship has been completely changed by Him.

All three, prophecy, priesthood and kingship are inseparably united in one person, Jesus Christ. These three stand opposed to all natural aspirations and efforts. Christ as such has power to break down that which stubbornly persists in man under the bondage of sin, and to renew him. He alone could meet challenge of Satanic powers. He as such has borne man's predicaments, and solved them in their depth.

But His way cannot be interpreted by man's standard. He must do according to His own plan. His concern is solely the salvation of mankind. And His saving activity flows out of love. When His love comes to act in this hate-filled world, its way surpasses all human expectations, even as people of His own day could not understand it. His love is creative love. It is not the expression of eros. For man's salvation this love spontaneously works through the three offices of Christ. It sometimes frustrates

man's efforts for freedom, as was the case with Judas. It sometimes gives unexpected hope for eternal life as was the case with
one of the criminals on the cross. The love of Christ changes
every human situation for good or for worse. We may say that
love is given, yet love is lost; love opens the eyes of men, yet
love blinds them. Love's action cannot be understood by philosophy, or psychology, or any other scientific research. This is
history, but not ordinary history. It is salvation history. The
revolutionary reconciliation is God's love in action on a universal
scale. Through this action the insurmountable barrier which
blocked the fellowship between God and man was broken down.
This decisive event not only opened the way to God's fellowship
with man, but also man's loving relationship with others. Something new has come into human society. This is the new age
brought about by the second Adam in the midst of the old age.

III

The revolt of the first Adam involved all of humanity in sin.
Its consequence was that death came upon Adam's descendants
without exception. But "God who is rich in mercy, out of the
great love with which he loved us, even when we were dead
through our trespasses, made us alive with Christ . . . and
raised us up with him, and made us sit with him in the heavenly
places in Christ Jesus, that in the coming ages he might show
the immeasurable riches of his grace in kindness toward us in
Christ Jesus" (Eph. 2:4-7). God's redemptive act by which man
is freed from the last enemy, that is, death, is thorough-going.
It begins with God's bountiful mercy, and ends with the perfect
communion with God through Jesus Christ our Lord and Savior.
The redemptive activity through Jesus Christ was attempted
and achieved in spite of the fierce opposition of all the forces
of destruction "while we were yet sinners." When redemption is
seen in the present situation, it may be said to be the divine

revolution in the midst of an age which is depicted as nihilistic or demonic.

This divine revolution is ours through faith, as St. Paul says "by grace you have been saved through faith: and this is not your own doing, it is the gift of God" (Eph. 2:8). Faith is not human knowledge resulting from the acceptance of certain historical facts. It is the response of God's loving and redemptive act. That answer is possible only at the same time that man is subdued by agape-love, and surrenders himself to God, the Father of Jesus Christ. Faith, therefore, means separation from one's own self and decisive choice for God. It is the revolution of an individual as initiated by the divine revolution. Therefore faith is characterized by venturesomeness or daring boldness. This audacious "faith comes from what is heard, and what is heard comes by the preaching of Christ" (Rom. 10:17). Faith is correlative with Christ, but the proclamation of the Gospel comes first.

Christ who holds the threefold office has dealt the fatal death-blow to the hostile powers, but still continues to struggle against them. The continuation of the work of Christ is done by the Holy Spirit. Wherever the Gospel is preached, there the Holy Spirit works mightily through the proclaimed word. The Holy Spirit who uses the Word and Sacraments as the means of grace breaks through to the citadel of sinful man, and convicts of sin until man acknowledges his unworthiness before God and confesses his egocentric attitude, seeking forgiveness.

When the proclamation of redemptive act of Christ leads man to repentance, there is forgiveness and life. Personal revolution within divine revolution takes place. He is now completely in Christ, and is a newly created and freed man; that is, a slave of righteousness instead of a slave of sin. This is really a Copernican revolution in man's life. Faith works this wonder. Faith alone is the channel which connects man to the life-giving fountain. Man is permitted to stand justified before God by faith alone. This is the eternal and precious truth revealed in the Scriptures, and treasured by Martin Luther. The new creature in Christ is free from sin, death and devil. He is no longer a slave in Satan but a slave in Christ. Luther's propositions in his "The Freedom of Christian Man" fits well at this point: "a Christian man is the most free lord of all, and subject to none; a Christian man is the most dutiful servant of all, and subject to every man." A Christian man is a Christ in Christ. Just as Christ is the most free lord of all so a man in Christ is the most free lord of all. Just as Christ is a humble servant of all, so a man in Christ is the most willing servant of all. Both lordship and servitude, which are apparently contradictory ideas, are realized in one and the same person Jesus Christ. What happens in Christ is also realized in man through faith in Him. The freedom through faith is the real freedom, as Jesus Christ says, "if the Son shall make you free, you shall be free indeed" (John 8:36).

In this connection we must remember that while we are free and justified in Christ, at the same time we are also still sinners subjected to the powers hostile to the divine will as long as we live in the world. Therefore it is necessary for us to learn the real significance of the Sacraments. Luther says in regard to the Baptism: "it signifies that the Old Adam in us should, by daily contrition and repentance, be drowned and die with all sins and evil lusts, and again, a new man daily come forth and arise, who shall live before God in righteousness and purity forever." The Christian life is the life of tension-filled struggle; a tension between death and resurrection. The Lord of Resurrection supplies the Christian with renewed power by means of the Lord's Supper. Again Luther explains its benefits, saying, "that is shown by these words, 'Given and shed for you for remission of sins'; namely, that in the Sacrament forgiveness of sins, life, and salvation are given us through these words. For where there is forgiveness of sins, there is also life and salvation."

Christ is the Lord of all Christians. Is He not also the Lord of all non-Christians? And again is He not the Lord over all the creation? If so, His struggle against the evil powers is not limited to the transforming work of man, but also concerns the setting up a new world order, although we are not permitted to interpret it by our own standards. But we live in hope to see "the new heavens and new earth."

Whatever temporal and critical circumstances may overwhelm us, one thing is certain—fellowship promised by Christ will continue as long as man continues to believe in Jesus Christ. Luther explains the relationship between Christ and His believer by using the picture of the marriage relationship. Christ as husband takes all things that belong to the believer, His wife. Luther says, "in this displayed the delightful sight, not only communion, but of a prosperous warfare, of victory, salvation and redemption." In this marriage all things that belong to Him become the possession of the believer, and all things of the believer become His. He shares in the sins, death and hell. And He deals with them "as if He himself had sinned; and when He suffers, dies, and descends to hell, that He may overcome all things, and since sin, death and hell cannot swallow Him up, they must needs be swallowed up by Him in stupendous conflict" (The Freedom of Christian Man). However, the full manifestation of our Christian freedom will be realized at the end of time when Christ returns. Then there we will know the real significance of freedom from law, sin, death and devil. We are now living in time between the beginning of the new age, and the consummation of His promise at His second coming. The freedom we have at present is fragmentary. But we have God's promise that this freedom in Christ shall be manifested in glory. Then the life in communion with God and the life together with our fellowmen will be consummated in glory and power. This glorious life together will not be restricted geographically nor racially nor socially. There will be no Jew nor Greek, no East nor West. All will be free because all will be one in Christ.

Dr. Hans-Werner Gensichen

A member of the Evangelical Church of Wuerttemberg in Germany, Dr. Gensichen is professor of church history and ecumenics at Gurukul Theological College in Madras, India. He is currently on leave from that position, to which he was named in 1955, to lecture on missions and comparative religion at Heidelberg University, Germany.

Born in 1915 in Hannover, Germany, he took his undergraduate study in Germany. He received his Master of Sacred Theology (S.T.M.) degree from Princeton Theological Seminary in 1938. He was awarded Doctor of Theology degree by Goettingen University, Germany, in 1942. He was ordained a pastor in the Evangelical Lutheran Church of Hannover in 1943. He was active in the military service 1938-45.

Between 1946 and 1952 he served as inspector of studies in two candidates' seminaries of the Hannover Church, later as secretary of the German Evangelical Missionary Council and then as lecturer in church history at the Church Faculty in Hamburg.

In 1952 he joined the faculty of the Divinity School of the Tamil Evangelical Lutheran Church in Tranquebar, India, then assumed his present post at Gurukul Theological College in Madras in 1955.

The Unity
of the Church
in Christ

I

OUR Lord Jesus Christ who has called us to freedom, also calls us to unity. As freedom, so also unity is present in Himself, *prior* to any effort on our part. But this unity exists also *for* us, both as a gift to be received and as a task to be accomplished. Our unity is to become an actual reality through the power of the Lord who is present among us in His Spirit, for "the dividedness of the church does violence to the Holy Spirit who lives in it" (F. C. Fry). This actualization requires more than correct but noncommittal theories and more than beautiful but ephemeral sentiments; it involves the total living reality of our churches. And if we should wish to ignore or resist the Lord's call, the fact remains that unity will be actualized nevertheless, but it will be *against* us.

Many voices today sound the call to unity; often, however, it is merely unity of fashion, or of strategy, or of ideology. Hence it is of the utmost importance that the churches listen to no other voice than their Lord's and respond to it in faith and in love. The manner in which this is done may vary according to time and circumstances. For instance, it is not necessary for the churches in Asia and Africa to develop their ideas of faith and obedience in exact conformity to the patterns of thinking current in the West. What is perfectly clear, however, is that the question of unity faces these young churches with unparalleled urgency. The following discussion will therefore frequently refer to their situation—in the hope that this look beyond the boundaries of our own local Lutheran churches may provide some needful and wholesome new insights into the question before us.

II

The church's unity is first of all, and above all, a matter of faith. In distinction from all human ideas of unity, our church's unity stands and falls with our faith in the one good Shepherd who calls His own together to be one flock, and does so in His own unique way. It has pleased Him to tie up His presence with the Word and the Sacraments which by the power of the Holy Spirit create faith and preserve it. Word and Sacrament are "the ministry of the message of reconciliation," the reconciliation with God that frees us from the bondage of sin but also calls us together and keeps us together in the fellowship of the reconciled in order that we should bring the message of reconciliation to the entire world.

When the Lord calls us to unity in faith, He first of all directs a question to us ourselves; for His call must under no circumstances be interpreted as suggesting that we may remain as we are and that only "the others" ought to change their mind. Are we not often dangerously close to demanding of others what we are not seriously willing to do ourselves? For instance, is it fair, when discussing doctrinal matters with other churches, to select

44

as a point of decisive difference some question on which there is
no complete unanimity within our own Lutheran family? Is it
fair to criticize others for confusing Law and Gospel when our
own skirts are by no means immaculate? Of course, we do not
wish to be perfectionistic; we have the duty of "testing the spir-
its," a duty that must not be postponed indefinitely or ignored
entirely. But nevertheless we need to remind ourselves of the
inherent danger of applying a double standard when measuring
deficiencies. We are always tempted—at least secretly—to identify
our own denomination with the Church of Christ. No church
"loses face" when it approaches the question of unity in a spirit
of fairness and honesty. For it is no human agency that addresses
us but the Lord Himself, who desires His Church to be one.
When Peter asked the Lord, "What about this man?" he was
told, "Follow thou me!" (John 21:21, 22.)

It is only after a heart-searching self-examination that we have
the moral right to approach others with reference to the unity
of the church. To be sure, we shall meet many divergent notions as to the right way to church-unity. Often there is no
willingness to place the problem of Word and Sacrament, of
confession and faith, into the center. We shall see later that
there are other important issues, but we must insist that this
is the basic problem; otherwise we would not be faithful to the
voice of our Shepherd. In plain terms this means that the only
way for the Lutheran church to approach the other churches is
the way of doctrinal discussion.

Let me recall some experiences from the discussions between
the Lutherans of South India and the Church of South India.
It may be that these actual events show more clearly than long
theoretical discussions what the issue really is. In the course of
the years the two parties have learned, on the one hand, that
certain basic questions of faith have a way of forcing themselves
again and again into the foreground; they simply will not allow

themselves to be disposed of by means of easy compromises or by an escape into a fictitious "unity transcending all differences." And, on the other hand, it has become clear that unity in faith and in the proclamation of the Gospel does not mean complete unity in theological interpretation and doctrine; kerygma and theology are two different things. Our conversations were most productive when there was no attempt to defend or attack certain theological positions or to impose definite formulations upon the other party, but when, jointly listening to the Scriptures and the church's witness, we sought in all humility to understand, or may I say, to spell out, word by word, what it is "that the Spirit saith to the churches," quite specifically to the actually existing churches in India today. Ultimately, the participants in these discussions discovered that this was a supremely valuable activity; for we were not concerned with defeating an enemy in a battle of scholastic definitions and distinctions, but with a joint witness to those *assertiones,* or basic convictions of faith, which Luther emphasized in his struggle against Erasmus the skeptic; in other words, we were concerned with those basic and relevant affirmations by which and with which a man may live and die, even the plain Christian man in an Indian village church.

It is a fairly general ecumenical experience that doctrinal discussions often fail to lead to better understanding or closer relations. Even the most elementary difficulties involved in the communication of ideas can be overcome only with a large quantity of patience, tact, and fairness. But this is no argument against holding doctrinal discussions. On the contrary, attempts to conduct discussions on doctrine must under no circumstances be abandoned—unless we are ready to admit that there is no escape from the sluggish warfare of confessionalistic self-preservation or from the indiscriminate notions of the advocates of union at any price.

If one raises the question what may be the outcome of all these

46

discussions, our Confession replies significantly, "Unto the true unity of the church it is sufficient to agree concerning the doctrine of the Gospel and the administration of the Sacraments" (Conf. Aug. vii). The theologian, in the privacy of his study, may note with satisfaction that wherever this statement is accepted, a common basis has been established for continued intensive discussion of theological problems. But this is not enough for the churches who are face to face with the burning urgency of the problem of unity. In the South India discussions there were deliberations on the question whether or not "visible external unity" is essential for the church. No doubt this question has a place in the discussions if it leads to the insight that even the most perfect institutional unity cannot possibly actualize in tangible perfection the essential unity of the church as the body of Christ. The question, however, involves a danger: it is possible to confuse what Luther called the "hiddenness of the church under the cross" with a conception of invisibility which is altogether idealistic or spiritualistic, and so to evade the practical implications of the Lord's call to unity. It goes without saying that genuine oneness of faith cannot be established, as it were, overnight, simply by an unanimous vote on some doctrinal statement. There are, as we all know, various stages in church-unity, and organizational union need not be the first stage. But as Lutherans we ought to know, that differences in liturgy or church policy or in the so-called non-theological factors do not permit us to side-step the question of external union on the basis of Articles vii and viii of the Augsburg Confession—unless there are absolutely compelling reasons why we should do so. It is an encouraging sign of the times that Lutherans are beginning to face this question in all seriousness, at least so far as inner-Lutheran relationships are concerned, for instance in America and Germany.

Our Lutheran emphasis on the priority of unity in faith has a negative side which often gives offence to non-Lutherans and may cause doubts to rise within our own ranks. The fathers of the Reformation said a very plain "No" to certain old and new heresies and on occasion even used the word *damnamus;* their purpose was to state unambiguously that in these particular respects there was no unity of faith. But today we would not act in accordance with our fathers' principles if we accepted all these boundary markers uncritically, without examination. Boundary lines are subject to change; some have vanished, new ones have been added. If it is true that the Lord of the church intends to unify His church through the preaching of the Word and the administration of the Sacraments, then there must be boundary lines also today, for the sake of the truth of the Gospel. These demarcation lines are not intended to furnish convenient labels to be applied to heretics but rather, at least primarily, they serve as sign posts and danger signals for the members of our church. The Confession drawn up by the Batak church shows that, and how, this may be done in our own day.

In this connection we must, at least briefly, touch the problem of communion-fellowship. Here, at the Table of the Lord, where the many should become one body by partaking of the one loaf, more nourishment has been given to divisiveness than anywhere else. Here, where the fellowship of the reconciled, united in heart and soul, was to proclaim the Lord's death until He return, our unity of faith is particularly grievously obstructed and broken. The situation is especially critical for the Lutheran Church. On the one hand, we Lutherans claim that our doctrine of the Lord's Supper approaches most closely the intentions of the Lord, and we have in the course of history drawn very sharp lines of distinction over against those who disagree with our doctrine. But, on the other hand, we ourselves are today perhaps farther than ever removed from complete agreement on the traditional Lutheran doctrine of the Lord's Supper. Today there is at least one Lutheran Church which has reached agreement on the Lord's Supper with its Calvinistic neighbor church, not

to mention various types of "emergency" intercommunion prac-
tised in diaspora regions or in young churches. There are Lutheran churches which "really see no obstacle" to intercommunion
with the Anglican Church. Some present-day Lutheran exegetes
assert that the Lutheran doctrine of the Lord's Supper as stated
in the Confessions, does not do full justice to the biblical witness. And then there are many other Lutherans who view all
this as deplorable apostasy from the faith of the fathers.

What should we do in this ominously obscure situation? Should
we not first of all humbly strive for a higher degree of unanimity
within our own ranks? How can we expect others to believe our
assertions when we do not live up to them in our own house!
At the same time, however, we must not allow the Lord's Supper to be misused as a mere means to external establishment
of church-unity; nor should we forget that sometimes the differences in the doctrine of the Lord's Supper are really only the
symptoms of still deeper doctrinal differences. Of course, it is
the Table of the Lord, and not ours, to which we are called;
and He is present, regardless of our interpretations of the mode
of His presence. But this does not exempt us from the duty, in
our teaching about the Lord's Supper and in our practice of
communion, to adhere strictly to the word of the Bible and the
will of Him who instituted it. For this reason we cannot favor
unlimited intercommunion, by means of which and as a result
of which doctrinal differences are—so it is hoped—to be overcome. The discussions in South India prove that an honest and
frank discussion concerning the Lord's Supper holds more promise than does any attempt to cover up existing differences by
compromise.

III

Christ has reconciled us to God and united us in the fellowship of the reconciled in order that each brother, as Luther put
it, may become a Christ to his brother. As faith is the basis of

this brotherhood so love is the power that lives and rules in it. The two are inseparable. It is true, of course, that the unity of the churches cannot be realized after the pattern of a love-marriage where the two parties simply follow their sentiments without considering all the other necessary prerequisites. Neverthless, we should remind ourselves that faith without love is dead and that the oneness of the church cannot remain alive and strong unless there is constantly renewed obedience to the "new commandment" which the Lord gave to His followers. Particularly when striving to achieve unity in faith, we must always seek after oneness in love; not as though love were a supplement or appendix to oneness of faith but because it is the fruit and the touchstone of its genuineness.

There was a time when non-Christians recognized the Christians "because they loved one another." Perhaps there are such instances even today. But by and large there is not much evidence of such love in our congregations today. At times it would appear as though unity in faith and confession now and then results in indifference over against unity in love. The Study Document poses the question, "Can churches with the same confession take it upon themselves not to be in church fellowship?" (The German version actually asks, Is there a defense for such action?) With the same show of reason one could ask, Is there a defense for Christians professing the same confession and not living together in the fellowship of love? Is it defensible when they permit their oneness in faith to be disturbed and disrupted by factors which have nothing to do with faith as such?

Just as in India the caste system, even among many Christians, still exercises a divisive role, so elsewhere in the world there are social and racial factors, national and linguistic differences which seriously obstruct the complete union of churches of the same confession. We shall see later that many of these natural or historical differences need not affect the unity of the church at all. Here we wish to emphasize, however, that such differences assume the character of questionable separatism when, e.g., in one and the same country two neighboring churches whose members have the same national background but use different languages, cannot find the road to unity and only too often treat each other with anything but love.

No one here would be presumptuous enough to assume the role of the impartial judge. We all, East and West, whether we are aware of it or not, are too frequently engaged in the business of erecting barriers which keep our oneness in faith from coming to fruition and which incidentally painfully encumber the relation between missions and young churches. Organizational procedures will avail nothing unless the power of spontaneous love overcomes these barriers and so gives to the existing unity of faith an opportunity of expressing itself in real life, in the heart and life of each believer.

Again, it is love that guards against the dangerous legalistic zeal of those who would seek to establish uniformity when there is unity in faith. The desire for uniformity is basically a kind of selfishness: everybody else must be formed in my image. But love does not seek its own. Love keeps the Gospel from relapsing into Law. Our fathers knew this; that is why they rejected uniformity in "ceremonies" and in church polity as a prerequisite for church unity. Love must be on guard so that there is no anti-evangelical coercion toward uniformity anywhere—among other reasons because "the strong ought to bear the infirmities of the weak and not to please themselves" (Rom. 15:10). A revival, for instance, can easily divide a church into two classes of Christians, a higher and a lower class. The "strong" will then have to examine themselves whether their love is as strong as their faith, and whether it is right for them to sacrifice the unity of the church to their own peculiar higher insights. The "weak" should examine themselves as to whether their attitudes do not perhaps compel the strong to leave the church. In such situations it is necessary that Christian love develop all its latent powers of patience, prudence, and vigilance in order to "keep the revival within the church," as was the case, for instance, in Hungary in the thirties, and as is so urgently necessary today in East Africa.

But the service of love is still more necessary, in fact, absolutely indispensable in all those situations where—while avoiding uniformity—unity in faith needs to be preserved in the face of differences which are either part of the natural equipment or the result of historic processes. In Christ we have the abolishment—not of the natural development of nations or languages but of the curse of mutual hatred and misunderstanding brought about by sin. The new people of God which is being collected by the Lord possesses a superior kind of unity which does not abolish these natural differences but does remove their divisive character. It is love's high office to preserve this "miracle of the church among the nations," particularly at the time when the nations are at each other's throats in their struggle for power. The traditional Lutheran tendency of preserving the natural linguistic, cultural, and social endowment of the people, if viewed from this perspective, is of some significance, especially in the world of young churches. It must be admitted, however, that during the period of transition from mission to young church, all too frequently our Lutheran missions were governed by the spirit of the West and the life patterns of western church. There is all the more reason, therefore, that now at last the western partners should exercise genuine love for the young churches and actively support (not merely passively stand by) the young churches as they establish their own forms of church life even when they are strange and inappropriate according to western traditions. Real sacrifices may be demanded of those who undertake to render this service of love; but the reward will be a deeper and richer experience of the unity of faith.

Unity in faith and unity in love belong together. Love alone is insufficient as a basis for the unity of the church. But love has the quality of looking and acting—with less restraint than faith—

beyond the boundaries of the church. Here we behold the vast field of interchurch cooperation in all those areas which do not touch our confession or faith. The portion of this activity which the Lutheran churches of the world have performed especially since the last war—from various kinds of relief activities to the Commission on International Affairs—need not be described here. It may even be that compared with full unity in confession and faith these achievements are relatively modest. But this is no reason to minimize their value: love is at work here, for Christ's sake, in its desire to help the brother. It may happen that in the exercise of such love, two churches of different confessions now and then approach one another so closely that one is tempted to speak of a preliminary step on the road to unity in faith. Who are we to assert, or to deny, this? What is important for us is to have the confidence that our Lord may lay His blessing upon such activities (even though theologically they may rate low) and that under His protection some little plant may grow (though hidden from our view) which eventually makes its contribution toward a more complete unity of faith. May there not be times when it pleases the Lord to bring His followers closer to the goal by teaching them the lessons of love in the school of joint suffering? The church struggle in Germany, or the prisons and concentration camps during the war and in the years after the war in all parts of the world will probably be recognized by future generations as milestones along the road to unity. The pressure directed here and there against the church today may lead some of the separate churches to approach one another more closely as they bear the cross which all of us have to carry, and suffer with another in genuine brotherly love.

IV

Our deliberations and discussions concerning the unity of the church dare not stop when we leave this meeting. God deals with His people in our complex world in the specific situation of each particular church. Here, in this concrete reality, the church must prove whether, and if so to what extent, it is willing to obey the Lord's call to unity. The co-existence of Christians of different confessions within one locality, or within one territory, may be considered as the practical testing area in those things which are being discussed and determined on the high-level doctrinal discussions. This is especially true in such localities where the dividedness of the church has become an offence to non-Christians and seriously jeopardizes the missionary testimony.

It is not accidental that in such situations mission and unity prove to be inseparable. In the local congregation, that is to say, in the weekday life of the mission church, the final inescapable test is made as to whether the church truly accepts the last will of the Lord, "that they all may be one . . . that the world may believe" (John 17:21). And in the last analysis it is here that the church will have to show whether it is chiefly concerned in preserving and justifying its own existence or in "reaching forward to those things which are before" (Phil. 3:17). The church should be the "pace-setter" for the coming kingdom which will usher in the consummation of the church's unity as well as its mission, when all the ecumenical problems will find their ultimate solution, including those that seem to defy solution, as the Roman schism and the ongoing process of the formation of new "sects."

It is only in the light of eternity that the problem of unity may be properly viewed in its depth and breath, its requirements and its promises. The warning of John the Baptist did not only apply to his contemporaries, but it also means us who will, one day, face Him when He returns as the Judge: "Think not to say within yourselves, we have Abraham to our father; for I say unto you, that God is able of these stones to raise up children unto Abraham." But the mightier One, whose coming the Baptist announced, is, we firmly believe, present with us to baptize us with the Holy Ghost and with fire. He shows us and our

54

churches the one and only way which has promise, the way which has been opened to us by His call to unity in the saving truth, namely, to be gathered by Him and to gather with Him. And so, at last, "there shall be one fold and one Shepherd" (John 10:16).

Bishop Bo Harald Giertz

Bishop Giertz has been spiritual leader of the Diocese of Goteborg (Gothenburg) in the Church of Sweden for the past eight years.

Born in Rapplinge, Sweden, in 1905, he is a graduate of the University of Uppsala (1928) and also studied in Rome and Jerusalem. Converted from radical atheism, he received his theology degree from Uppsala in 1931.

He served as executive secretary of Christian High School Movement (1932-35). He was named pastor in the Diocese of Linkoping in 1935 and served most of the time in a small parish in Torpa (1938-49). During this time he produced several theological works and novels. In 1943 he was appointed Chaplain to the King, an honorary title. Five years later he was made the first choice of pastors in the Gothenburg Diocese for the post of bishop and a year later, in 1949, received the appointment.

His wide travels include a lecture tour in the U.S. in 1953.

Freedom to Reform the Church

O N THE stormy coasts in my home diocese you can see the oaks drawing themselves together in the shelter of rocky heights and twisting themselves into thickets of writhing trunks. Seen from a distance such trees bear little resemblance to the giant shade-trees that spread their branches in solitary majesty on inland meadows. But study them closer and you will find the same leaves and the same acorns. An oak is always an oak.

So it is with the Church. At first sight there doesn't seem to be much resemblance between the early Jerusalem church, the church of Ambrose in Milan, Luther's church in Wittenberg, or our own churches in Gothenburg or Minneapolis. At different times the Church may appear in different forms. Yet it is the same Church. A Christian is always a Christian.

The form of the oak is determined by forces placed in its seed by the Creator. The Church, wherever it is found and in whatever form, is the result of a creative and shaping power given it by God as its source and its nourishment.

This formative power is the Holy Spirit, whose visible and tangible tools are the Word, and the Sacraments. On this account Augustana declares that where the Word is rightly proclaimed and the sacraments rightly administered there the Church exists (CA, VII, cf. Apology VII). If this be not rightly done the Church languishes or dies. But where the Gospel is proclaimed in biblical purity and the sacraments are administered according to Christ's institution, there is the Church, however varied the external forms may be because of national traits and historical circumstances. All these branches grow from the one root, out of the one trunk. The fruit they bear is one. A Christian is always a Christian. Christianity is always a faith in Christ the Savior, a faith that works in love.

Our Lutheran Churches are convinced that they belong to the one, holy, catholic, apostolic Church. The Augsburg Confession concludes with the confident assertion that neither in doctrine or in ceremonies have we accepted anything against Scripture or the Church Catholic. We hold firmly to that claim. Not that we make of the early church a law to be followed in the ordering of the Church for all time to come. But we believe that the Spirit of God created the ancient Church and that its dogma of the Triune God expresses the truth of Scripture. The Bible teaches us to speak of Abraham as *our* Father (Luke 2:73, Romans 4:16). In the same manner we can speak of *our* apostles and *our* great church fathers.

But we speak also of *our* Reformers, confident that the same Spirit used them to purify and renew the apostolic Church. We believe also that the same Spirit through the same Gospel seeks to be our life, our light and our guide.

Of this, then, we are sure, that there really is a Church which stands through the ages. There is a continuity of the Church. All the biblical images of the Church assert it. The Church is the new Israel. A people endures from generation to generation. The Church is the body of Christ. A body does not exist only for a moment. The Church is a building, a temple of the Spirit. A house remains where it stands, from year to year. True Christianity consists not only in hearing the Word, but in continuing in the Word (John 8:31). Christ continues in us and lives in us.

The Holy Spirit dwells in us. It is certain that with human eyes we cannot discern where the true life in Christ is present and who are the true members. But it is equally certain that the true Church, the body of Christ, is actually present in the world and continues from age to age as truly as my body persists from this day to the next. Our human drowsiness and indifference does not destroy this continuity. Even the wise virgins slept, but they did have oil in their lamps.

So the Church is a living organism. It has, thus, both that which abides and is unchangeable and that which grows, is consumed and renewed.

There is in the Church that which can never be reformed or changed. Such is the Gospel and "the faith which was once delivered unto the saints" (Jude 3). No authority in the Church has the power to alter the smallest letter in this Gospel. If it tries, it ceases to be an authority in the Church and is subject to Scripture's inexorable: "Let him be anathema" (Gal. 1:8ff).

Here there can be no willingness to compromise. Usually it is just this unchangeable which the world wants to reform. It wants to polish away what moralistic reason considers blemishes on the beauty of the Church. Why should salvation depend only on grace, only on Jesus, only on faith? Surely a good will, moral blamelessness, religious fervor must count for something in the eyes of God. Why are the Word and Sacrament so important? Are there not various ways to God?

To all such suggestions to reform the message of the Church and its manner of work, the Church must reply simply, "No, Jesus is the Way, the Truth, the Life. No one comes to the Father but through Him. Faith comes of preaching. This is my beloved Son. Hear Him." So the Lord says, and the Church cannot say otherwise.

So if we ask what it is in the Church which endures by divine law, Augustana replies first and foremost: the Gospel (CA XXVIII). Furthermore, the other means of grace—baptism, the Lord's Supper, absolution. Also, the office of the ministry, instituted by God. Finally, we teach "that *one,* holy Christ is to continue forever" (CA VII). Here the Confession draws the boundary line. The outward institutions of the Church exist "lure humano," i.e., they are shaped by human law. It is regulated by human ordinances, rites, and ceremonies, instituted by men (traditiones humanae, ritus, ceremoniae ab hominibus institutae). In such matters the Church acts in freedom.

The ordering of the preaching ministry is one of the factors subject to variation. The Reformers clearly saw that the episcopacy was not in apostolic times what it later became. Yet they did not object to its retention. Customs of the apostolic age are not a law for ours. For instance, we are not bound by the apostolic council's decision to abstain from blood. A human ordinance can and should be continued as long as it serves a good purpose. The Spirit of God creates and fashions the Church. God's will can find expression in an historical development. Therefore some of our churches have retained the episcopal office of the early Church.

Motivations can vary. The Apology (on Augustana XIV) asserts that "it is our greatest wish to maintain Church polity and the grades in the Church, even though they have been made by human authority. For we know that Church discipline was instituted by the Fathers, in the manner laid down in the ancient canons, with a good and useful intention."

The Swedish Church Order of 1571 went a step farther, declaring "this order was very useful and undoubtedly came from God the Holy Spirit (the giver of all good gifts)," wherefore it "was favored and adopted all over Christendom, and has ever since continued, and will last as long as the world stands." These words of the Church Order (written by our first evangelical archbishop) do not mean, of course, that the episcopal order is necessary for a right administration of the means of grace. It is a good order and a good gift of God, and is expected to remain for all time. But if any one were to make of this matter of convenience a matter of salvation by saying that there cannot be true ministers and true sacraments unless there are bishops, all our churches would rise up in unanimous protest.

From this follows our attitude toward the matter of apostolic succession. We may value it as one of the many visible proofs of our connection with the Church of the apostles. We may restore it, if it is broken, in the same way as we can restore the communion liturgy of the early Church when it has fallen into disuse. But it can never be a question of compulsion, of something that *has* to be. The practice of the Swedish Church is an illustration. This Church is one of those Churches which are considered to be in possession of apostolic succession. It prizes this possession and rejoices over the opportunities for ecumenical contacts which it affords. But at the same time this Church receives as a matter of course, pastors from other Lutheran Churches who do not have the Succession and considers their ordination without any question as a valid ordination.

It is conceivable that new confessional writings may become necessary, not to replace those we now have, but to supplement them. The Confessions are not a compendium of Scripture, a summary of all our faith. They make a powerful witness to the Evangelical faith, and they give more precise expression to this faith and define its limits on those points to which attention had been drawn by the conflict of the time. The questions around which controversy raged in the 16th century are not always the questions in which our time finds itself in greatest need of guidance. Especially in cases where the Church establishes itself in an heathen environment or in a radically changed cultural world we can readily imagine the necessity of formulating its position in new articles. These then become a standard around which to rally and which leads the way to an unknown future. Our Swedish Church Order of 1571 was this kind of a confession. Such new Confessions need not be adopted necessarily by all Lutheran Churches. It is enough that we hold to those we already have. They give evidence of our faithfulness to the Credo of the Early Church and the truth of the Gospel as our Reformers have helped us to understand them. On this foundation each one may then have freedom to say whatever needs be said in any age and any part of the world.

The freedom of the Church in every period to order its life in the most effective way is maintained very clearly in the Formula of Concord (SD:X). The Church of God has power and authority to determine anywhere and any time, when circumstances warrant, to change all so-called adiaphora, that which pertains to its external functioning, its order of worship, its form of organization, its various ministries, its congregational constitution and its methods of work. The Confession defines these adiaphora as "ceremonies and Church rites which are neither commanded nor forbidden in God's Word, but are introduced into the Church with a good intention, for the sake of good order and propriety, or otherwise to maintain Christian discipline" (in opening section of Ch.X).

In the same article the Formula of Concord gives a classic statement of the principle to be followed in all reform efforts, namely, to effect what "at any time may be regarded as most profitable, most beneficial and best for (preserving) good order, (maintaining) Christian discipline (and for eutaxia worthy of the profession of the Gospel), and the edification of the Church."

The Church must not lose its freedom to change its forms of functioning. There are good things, including even treasures of the church, which wear out and in time have to be replaced. For instance, Bible translations, hymn books and catechisms. These too must change when language and environment change. To a certain extent this is true, also, of church buildings and architecture which follow changes in building materials and techniques. The Church always has to contend with an egocentric conservatism which insists that everything shall be as it was only because people are accustomed so to have it. This kind of conservatism is not evangelical. It is the kind that has fastened on the Roman Church its unintelligible language and its unalterable liturgy. We of the Evangelical Church must not permit our old Bible translations, our old hymns, or our venerable pulpit language to become a new church-Latin.

True loyalty to the Gospel always means, therefore, to let the Spirit begin His creative work. Faithfulness to the Word is not loyalty to a rigid and finished institution by a participation in a creative activity wherein God is at work.

Therefore Paul writes to Timothy, "Guard the truth that has been entrusted to you by the Holy Spirit who dwells within us." We must have the Spirit if we are to be faithful stewards of talents entrusted to us. The Spirit enlightens also by imparting wisdom and making it possible for us to "prove what is the will of God, what is good and acceptable and perfect" also in matters that pertain to the building up of the Church and re-ordering of the Church's work in new and difficult circumstances. It is evidence of the Spirit's working through the Word when the Church constantly attacks new difficulties arising in its development, and when Christians carefully consider with each other matters that call for discussion in an attitude of constant prayer and ceaseless listening to the Word.

Again, Scripture provides examples. The letters of the Apostles represent an unceasing wrestling with ever new difficulties. Unforeseen problems crowd in on every side. The congregations ask questions. Sometimes they act without asking, and are in danger of going in a wrong direction. The Apostle gives counsel and exhortation. He points to the words of the Lord or quotes from the Old Testament. He gives his own opinion. In some cases he gives detailed instructions, in others he speaks only in general terms. But this constant wrestling with something new shows the Spirit at work in the Word.

It is ever so in the living Church. True, the age of the Apostles was a period of breaking through and building up, and everything had to be arranged, from the ground up. Today the younger Churches are in almost exactly the same situation. But even the older Churches are in a period of fateful transition. It would be a mistake to believe that the Apostles have given a final answer to all the problems of the Church, or an authoritative answer to all the practical problems that may arise. Such is the position of a false biblicism which Luther and the Reformers rejected. This is clear from the fact that we Lutherans have never looked on the rules which the Apostle Paul gave for a series of particular problems as binding on us. We do not have the same order of presbyters, bishops, and deacons as is mentioned in the pastoral epistles. We do not enroll as widows of the congregation women who are at least 60 years of age and have been married only once. Yet even such a portion of the Word of God can teach us something. It can point us in certain directions and give us counsel. It teaches us above all that the Church of God in matters of outward organization and methods of work never is finished but must always be prepared to serve the age in which it lives. In one place Paul gives Timothy certain directions about a minister's attitude towards money and adds, "Think over what I say, for the Lord will grant you understanding in everything" (2 Tim. 2:7). The Apostle knows how difficult it is to give a rule that covers all eventualities. He knows how hard it is to apply a principle. But he knows also that the Lord Himself will give understanding to His servant in each situation, to enable him to become a faithful and wise steward and to find the right solution in those unforeseen problems he will meet. When God's love (Rom. 5:5) has been poured into our hearts through the Holy Spirit, then indeed God can teach us to love God with all our mind, as the first and greatest commandment teaches us. The Lord has need even of such service. It would be a serious matter and a sign of stagnation if there were no questions in the Church, and there were no discussions of how to act, work, and speak. The Spirit would have ceased to work if everything were completed and closed. Then an unalterable tradition would have decided and regulated what God had reserved for decision and regulation by His Spirit. Then tradition would have assumed a role that belonged only to the Word and the Spirit.

The right to reform does not mean an itching eagerness to change. Two considerations obligate us to be cautious.

The one is the fact that the Holy Spirit has been at work also in the past. The human regulations in the Church are not *only* human. At the first council of the Church, following discussion and study of the Word of God, a unanimous agreement was arrived at and the process explained in these words, "it has seemed good to the Holy Spirit and to us." This does not imply that such decisions are binding on all ages. But it does suggest that we should always treat carefully the heritage of the Church. Especially in the matter of liturgy, as for example, in the communion service, the Holy Spirit has given us forms which have proved themselves vital even after a thousand years. They may turn out to be useful even to the day when Christ returns.

The other reason for caution is love. The Confessions constantly remind us that Scripture commands us to be concerned about weak brethren, that is, such as have difficulty when their devotion has to live and grow in new forms. Then, too, we must be anxious about unity. Harmony, says the Apology (on CAXV, toward end) is more important than all other advantages if it can be obtained without offense to consciences. In our time this matter of harmony in Church rites, in liturgy and hymns, has gained new significance because of the reducing of distances and the great increase in the number of emigrants and refugees to be cared for. For many thousands of people who must leave their homeland and Church, perhaps never to return, it is of great help if our churches can have so much in common that these people feel at home wherever they take part in evangelical-Lutheran worship.

Love, however, demands not only that we care for those who are used to a certain tradition. It demands also that we regard those who have *not* grown up in any church tradition at all.

This can happen in the old Churches. In various places those active in the Church have become a small minority in the great folk-Churches. These who sustain the work of the Church must then remember that the Church is not only for them. They cannot hold fast to what which they have loved and been accustomed to since childhood in such a way that each new generation becomes ever more alienated from the churchly heritage.

It is even more true of the younger Churches which are a fruit of missions in recent times. The old Churches have sometimes sinned against these by bringing to them, along with the Gospel, all the customs, usages and forms of thought which we in the Western world are accustomed to associate with the life of our Churches. We have shown ourselves in the mission fields exactly in the character we have developed here at home, with all those traits which can be understood only from our own particular history, and with all those controversial theological questions which once upon a time were of importance to us. At times we have forgotten that some of the things we have cherished have lost their importance even for people in our own land and become an obstacle in our effort to reach our own brethren. What can then be expected in the mission-field? Assuredly there are times when we need to say to each other what Peter said to the Apostles and the Elders in Jerusalem. "Now therefore why do you make trial of God by putting a yoke upon the neck of the disciples which neither our fathers nor we have been able to bear?" (Acts 15:10.)

On that occasion the Church saw its way clearly. A Greek or an Egyptian did not have to become a Jew in order to become a Christian. The road is the same today. An African or an Asian does not have to assume Western ways, forms of thought, or Western music and architecture, in order to become a Christian. In this matter we need to make clear to our brothers, with sympathy and with emphasis, what our confessional writings teach: The Church of God has power and authority in every time and every place to change churchly customs to the best advantage.

66

We would look to our colored brethren for those saintly, good, strong and wise church men who could take leadership in their hands and in love to their people arrange the life of the Church in their generation and among their countrymen in a way best suited "for (preserving) good order, (maintaining) Christian discipline (and for eutaxia worthy of the profession of the Gospel), and the edification of the Church."

The Church is the creation of the spirit and the temple of the Spirit. But where the Spirit of the Lord is, there is freedom. Just because it is the Spirit that builds the Church, it really grows, changes, adapts itself to new times, and yet remains the Church as long as it is faithful to the Word and Sacraments. The result is, on the one hand, a sound conservatism, a veneration of what we have inherited from our forefathers, a love to our churchly heritage, and, on the other hand, a humble willingness constantly to re-examine, an obligation in every age to seek to improve, and an unfearing confidence in the Spirit's guidance in new, strange situations.

It is a great gift of God that our Reformers had this insight and that our Lutheran confessional writings so clearly testify to it. Now we pray that this gift may belong to all our various Lutheran Churches, so that in all our conduct we may bear witness before the world to this freedom and this unity. Then we can truly be completely united in a common evangelical faith, and at the same time be generously tolerant in matters of churchly rites and ceremonies, giving to each what it desires. All the while we will love each other, understand the difficulties one of another, bear each other's burdens and strengthen each other's faith.

Dr. Edgar M. Carlson

Dr. Carlson has been president of Gustavus Adolphus College at St. Peter, Minnesota, since 1944. It is a school of the Augustana Lutheran Church.

Born in Amery, Wisconsin, in 1908, he is a graduate of Gustavus Adolphus and of Augustana Theological Seminary at Rock Island, Illinois. Ordained in 1933 and served as pastor of Mt. Olivet Lutheran Church in Minneapolis (1933-37), during which period he also attended the University of Minnesota. He served on the faculty of Gustavus Adolphus (1937-42) and on the faculty of Augustana Theological Seminary (1942-44). He received his Ph.D. from the University of Chicago in 1944.

He has served on numerous U.S. and world church groups, including Advisory Committee on the main theme for the Second Assembly of the World Council of Churches at Evanston, Illinois, in 1954. He was president of Augustana Luther League in 1948, president of National Lutheran Educational Conference in 1953 and president of Minnesota Association of Colleges in 1954.

Free for Service
in the World

W E WHO are gathered in Minneapolis these days as representatives of the Lutheran Church throughout the world are keenly aware that we must keep our eyes firmly fixed upon Him who is the Head of the Church. Unless we have "the mind of Christ" we are not likely to speak significantly to our world and time. We must focus our attention upon Him if we are to catch His vision of the world.

It is not in spite of this centrality of Christ in our thought, but because of it, that we must speak about our service to the world. He whom we know as Lord and Savior is the Lord and Savior of the world. If we would belong to Him in hallowed intimacy we must stand ready to be the agents of His love in faithful obedience to the ends of the earth. Nor dare we forget that it was part of that renewal of the Church which God granted through Luther and the Reformers that Christian discipleship is not a cloistered thing to be practiced in isolation from the world but is rather to be expressed in wholehearted engagement in the world of which we are a part.

It may be well for us to remember that the world is listening, too, to what we are saying these days. Unity and freedom are part of the vocabulary in which the world gives expression to its human hopes. Something there is in all of us that knows we were meant for unity and brotherhood and not for loneliness and enmity. We may not understand the full depth of the tensions that threaten our life together, we may be quite wrong about their causes or their cures, but our very humanity shrinks in terror from the thought that they should be permitted to grow unhindered and unchallenged until they reap their full harvest of tragedy again. And freedom, too, is a magic word that strikes a responsive chord in the human family. We may be quite wrong about our conception of freedom, we may seek it in unlikely places, and we may end in the most despairing servitude, but we will be disappointed and frustrated in our failure as those who were not meant to fail.

In that which follows we shall attempt to do three things: First, we will seek briefly to describe the Christian free man in order that we may approach our task with the same understanding of what it means to be free. Second, we will seek to describe a Christian view of the world in order that we may have a common understanding of the place in which our service is to be rendered. Third, we will seek to clarify certain aspects of the Christian's service to the world, particularly in relation to specific problems and issues which confront us in our time.

1. The Christian Free Man

First, then, who is the Christian free man? He is not just a man who has gained some measure of success in the universal quest for human freedom. He may or may not be living in a free society, with democratic forms of government. He may or may not be living in a land of abundance and opportunity. To be sure, the Christian free man is a man, and as such longs for freedom from tyranny and oppression, freedom from hunger and want, freedom from disease and pain, freedom from those limitations which are placed upon him by his own ignorance and weakness or from the inconsiderate will and evil intention of others in the society about him. But he is not distinguished from his fellows by the amount of such freedom he enjoys now or is likely to enjoy in the future.

It is at quite a different level that Christian freedom begins. The Christian has been made free. He has it as a gift and not as an achievement. Indeed, one would have to say that there is a freedom which the unbeliever claims which the Christian has surrendered—the freedom from God. To want to order one's life as though he were the center of the universe, as though there were no other god than one's own desires and ambitions and hopes—this the Christian knows as bondage and slavery. He knows that he cannot overcome the God whose world this is and whose law governs him as it does all men and things. He has known the might of God's hand upon him and felt the inescapable judgment of His law upon what he does and what he is, and he knows that there is no escape from it. The easy way of denying God's existence and the harder way of meeting His demands so as to be free of Him have become impossible alternatives for the Christian. The only way open is the way of surrender to this God whom he cannot escape. To this broken and defeated man, the God who has made Himself known in Jesus Christ speaks the reconciling and forgiving word, "Thy sins are forgiven thee." To hear and accept that word of forgiveness is to be made free. It is to have the center of one's life changed; it is to be governed by a center outside oneself, in God. It is to have been reconciled to God and to His world. It is to become a citizen of that kingdom to which we rightly belong. Indeed, it is to be righteous, for to be in this relationship of faith and trust, of acceptance and obedience, is to be in the right relationship to God.

So one can say that the Christian free man has been freed from himself in so radical and fundamental a way that he must be called a "new Creature." The difference between egocentric,

71

self-reliant, self-confident, and self-satisfied men and those whose trust and confidence is in Christ is the most radical and fundamental distinction that can be drawn between men.

It is important to remember, however, that the forgiven sinner never reaches a point where he no longer needs forgiveness. It is just in the acceptance of forgiveness that he transcends and overcomes his egocentricity. When he accepts forgiveness he is freed also from sin and guilt. By that same forgiveness, so dearly purchased and so firmly assured by Christ's death on the Cross, he has also been made free from the Law and from the wrath of God. Even death has lost its terror and its power through the triumph of God's utter love in Christ's death and resurrection from the dead. The Christian free man is thus a new man, standing in a new relationship to God, with a new perspective of his destiny and with a new outlook upon his world.

II. The Christian View of the World

What shall we say about the world which the Christian free man is called to serve? We must say that it is God's world. He created it and maintains it. It is not only true that He was the Creator; He is the Creator still. This day is as dependent upon His creative power as the first day. Our God is a living God, who moves and acts in all the processes of nature and of history. We are not less dependent upon Him today than was Abraham, though we may be less aware of our dependence. Because there is so much about the world of things which bears the mark of man's effort and inventive genius, and so much about our social institutions that has been willed into existence by the decisions of men, we may be deceived into thinking that this is our world; that we have taken the place of God as its creators. But we can still only discover and use the elements of the physical world; we cannot create them. For all we know about life and living things we cannot bring life into being. This is still God's world. This means much more than that He has given us laws according to which men are to govern themselves and use the world in which He has placed them. It means that His law is written into the very universe itself. In the physical world it has long been clear that nature is not subject to pure whim and fancy but that there is a certain necessity about it so that it is meaningful even in this day to speak of the "laws of nature." In the realm of human relations and social institutions, also, it is evident that there is at least a certain structure from which men cannot free themselves. There is biological necessity, for instance, for the existence of the family. The propagation of the race depends upon it. And within communities there must be some kind of political organization which maintains a degree of law and order among the members of the community. Physical hunger calls for some kind of economic activity and, in developed societies at least, some kind of economic organization. It is not accidental that men have been thrown into relationship of dependence and responsibility, in families and political units and economic societies. It could not be otherwise. The Christian, and particularly the Christian who has been instructed by Luther, sees in these structures and processes the on-going activity of God. They are "masks of God," he said. We live within these structures as a part of the discipline of God. For Luther the Law of God was not a set of legal statutes nearly so much as it was the concrete representative of law and order—the policeman, the school teacher, the parent. Even when such representatives are not Christian, or God-fearing, they are used of God in maintaining life and some degree of restraint upon self-centered men. It is part of God's gracious design that even evil men in the performance of their duties within society make some contribution to the common good.

The importance of what has been said above for the subject with which we are dealing is that the world in which we are called to serve is a world in which God is already at work. God's entrance into human affairs does not begin with our entrance into them. It will not do, therefore, to think of Luther or of the

Lutheran Church as belonging to the "world-denying" religions of the world. Neither will it do to think of the world of nature and history and society as a kind of neutral world, raw material, out of which we may make something good if we are good enough. It is not true that God's only point of contact with the world is the Christian and that the only power of God at work in the world is the power of the Gospel. There is a secular dominion of God which is not only represented by a claim on the part of God but is represented in the disciplines of life itself. When the Christian goes out to serve the world, he goes not into a strange and foreign land but into a dominion of God, as an obedient subject and a willing servant.

The Law according to which God exercises His dominion in the world and which is written into the very nature of the universe has been concretely formulated in the Ten Commandments, and most especially in the second table of those Commandments. There is a very intimate connection between the basic structures of society and the Commandments which stand guard against the disintegration of the family, the destruction of life, and disorder in the realm of human relations and property. Each of them protects and preserves some natural bond in the social body. The only complete fulfillment of this Law is in love like that which was revealed and incarnate in the person of Jesus Christ. As one who has been the object of the forgiving love of God in Christ, the Christian knows the real meaning of God's law of love which is at the heart of the universe itself.

The Law of God is all one, though it may demand different things of us in different relationships. Toward God the proper response of love is faith, trust, acceptance. Toward our neighbor it is forgiveness and helpfulness. As a parent it may involve discipline as well as forgiveness. For all in authority it involves the proper discharge of those functions which are the safeguards of the rights of others and which will result in the greatest good for all. In all of our human relationships God's Law requires that men shall always be governed by a sincere concern for their fellows and that they shall apply all their resources of mind and heart and will to know what things will contribute to their neighbor's good and to do them. This obligation rests alike upon all men, but the Christian knows that this is so.

One thing more must be said about this world in which the Christian is called to serve. There is an enemy at work in it. We need not seek far to find him, for he is in each of us. In man's own rebellious spirit—in the desire to usurp God's place as the sovereign of 'his own life and of at least as much of the world as affects him, is the real destructive power in all human society. This egocentricity, this bondage to ourselves, is in fact bondage to the devil, for it is this rebellion against God which the devil seeks to promote. We cannot fashion a world which will make men free from this bondage to themselves. Only God through His Law and Gospel can accomplish that release. The Christian can be the instrument of that Law and Gospel—to confess it and proclaim it and live by it. But when freedom comes to another as when it came to him, the Christian will know that it is God's gracious deed and not the product of any human service, even if it be that of a Christian free man.

III. The Christian's Service to the World

We shall now speak more specifically about the Christian's service to the world. First we shall make two general observations about it and then turn to problems and issues which confront the Christian in his service to our present time. The first observation is this: Because the Christian has been made free by God's free gift, and not by anything that he has earned for himself, he is free to serve his neighbor for his neighbor's sake. He does not need to keep his eye focussed on the reward which such service may bring, either in this world or in the world to come. Justification by grace alone, through faith alone, makes it possible for us to put our neighbor in the center. We are not

75

governed by legalistic rules but by human needs. We can and must be practical in our approach to the problems of our world. In every situation the Christian is free to choose the course of action which he honestly believes will result in the greatest good for his fellowmen. This practical aspect of the Lutheran understanding of Christian responsibility has far-reaching implications.

The second observation is this: Because God is already at work in the world of nature and history and social institutions, the Christian is free to work with all men and for all men. He can seek the welfare of others in community projects, in political organizations, in social welfare programs, in the councils of nations, and wherever else the opportunity may present itself, and do so from a genuine concern for his neighbors, even when those associated with him are not acting on the basis of such motivation. The real question is not whether we shall cooperate with those who do not share our faith and love but whether we shall cooperate with God who is at work in all the secular domains of life, even among those without faith and love.

And now we come to what may be the most difficult part of this assignment. What shall we say about the Christian's service in the face of particular and specific problems and issues which confront our world and time? From what has been said about the practical aspects of a Lutheran's understanding of the Christian's responsibility, it is clear that we cannot assume that the needs of men which lay their claim upon the Christian will be everywhere the same, except that all men need to be reconciled to God and all of us must be the willing witnesses of the saving Gospel. Even so, the strategy of our witness may vary. In those legitimate worldly needs which God wants us to have a share in supplying, the variation will be much greater. In a nation embarrassed by its abundance our needs are not likely to be the same as those in countries from which some of you come where hunger is a constant companion of many. In a land where people have so long enjoyed civil freedom that they have grown careless of it, the problems may be different than they are in countries where freedom is struggling to be born, or where it has been lost again. And to whatever extent the needs of the world about us differ, the claims which the neighbor's need makes upon the Christian will differ too. And still there are some things that we can say together and which we may need to say together in order to help us meet these varied claims.

1. The faithful fulfillment of our earthly callings, whether it be in the most simple society or the most highly technical and industrial civilization, constitutes an opportunity for doing something that God wants done in the world. If our job is not that kind of a job we ought not be in it. If it is that kind of a job we should do it well, for the sake of our neighbor. One must justify his existence in a society by doing something that contributes to the welfare of all.

2. We stand today in awe before the secrets of nature which have been unlocked by the genius of men of science and before the machines which have been produced by engineering skill. There are those among us who sometimes wonder whether this great body of scientific knowledge and engineering skill, which is now sufficient to destroy the human race, is not a measure of man's proud rebellion against God rather than a mark of God's presence in the world. But if what we have said about the world is true—that this is really God's world and that He is at work within it according to law—then the Christian may surely believe that God's hand is in all of this, even when He has had to work through men who knew Him not, and even though such expanding human knowledge involved the risk that it might be used by men against one another instead of for the welfare of all. The Christian may accept, use, and contribute to such scientific development in the confidence that this, too, is within the purposes of God for the world.

3. What shall one say about the struggle for freedom and for the establishment of political and social institutions suitable to its achievement? It may seem presumptuous for one who enjoys the full freedom which the Constitution of the United

77

States provides to instruct those among you for whom freedom is more hope than reality, but I should like to suggest some considerations which seem to me to be related to our Christian faith about the free man and about the world in which he lives.

a) God has been at work in the political structure of the world during all these centuries and there is reason for believing that His power is on the side of freedom. Despite the return of tyranny and oppression in some parts of the world in recent decades, the long trends of political history have been toward democratic structures rather than away from them. While the existence of government is ordained of God, it does not follow that any particular kind of government can claim the same kind of divine sanction which applies to government as such. The fact that God was able to use the absolute monarchy of King Solomon or the imperial rule of the Caesars does not imply any endorsement of absolute monarchy or imperial rule. Even Luther's "Letter to the Christian Nobility" must now be translated into a "Letter to the Citizens of Minnesota" if we are to claim his sanction for our views of Christian responsibility in a State.

There is reason for believing that God wills the increase of freedom, too, in the very nature of the Christian faith. For Christianity is a very personal religion—one man alone with God. No family, no nation, no Church can answer for any man in the presence of God. He must answer for himself. It is difficult to understand how a form of government in which the rulers prescribe what is demanded of the citizens, except insofar as such prescription is necessary to protect the rights of all, can do justice to the intensely personal way in which God deals with man in faith. Moreover, the Christian is called to serve his neighbor freely, out of genuine concern for him, and a good government must be such as to allow for the largest measure of such voluntary and generous action.

b) What the Church has to say in the matter of political freedom may need to be said differently to those who are in authority and to those over whom they rule. To those in authority, at national and international levels, surely the word of the Church must be in support of extending the areas of freedom. In some cases this may mean the establishment and promotion of programs which will prepare a people for the exercise of the rights and responsibilities of civil liberty. The direction and the goal should be clear. The Church must, also, remind those in authority that they are responsible to God, whether or not they are, also responsible through democratic processes to their own citizens. The Church may too easily accept the status quo, especially if it enjoys security within it. Those who profit from things as they are may be as selfish as those who rebel against them. The Church must be sure that it is not among them.

The word of the Church to those who seek a larger measure of freedom than the political structure now allows is more difficult. That they should be encouraged to use such lawful processes as may be at hand may be agreed by all. That they must be motivated in their concern for larger freedom by the welfare of all is also apparent. But what shall they do when governments under which they live do not provide for that minimum of freedom which is essential to human dignity and to the development of human personality? Christians cannot be indifferent to such a situation whether it is an accomplished fact in a government which has taken away civil freedom or a tendency within a government which threatens to end in such a result. *They must take positive action in the face of it.* This action may be in the form of patient suffering, consciously accepted. More than one tyranny has found the patient suffering of the "terrible meek" to be its greatest obstacle. Such action may be in the form of non-cooperation without violence—a weapon in behalf of freedom which is gaining stature and achieving results in more than one part of the world. It may be in the form of positive action to substitute order with freedom for oppressive domination. *When such a course of action is accepted as a last resort it must be in the name of true order and honest*

*government, and in behalf of the welfare of all, not as a private
action*. The decision with regard to which course is to be taken
in the face of such intolerable circumstances must be made by
the individual Christians, with full respect for the free decision
of others. Whatever alternative is chosen, those who suffer the
loss of freedom and react positively in the face of it are entitled
to the sympathetic understanding and support of Christians
everywhere.

4. Next to the proclamation of the Gospel itself, the service
to the world which has been particularly the Christian domain
has been the work of mercy. The Church's works of mercy have
been among the brightest jewels in her crown. This must always
be the case. As long as there are sick, poor, hungry, naked, home-
less, and imprisoned among our neighbors throughout the world
the Church and the individual Christian must heed their call.
Lutheran World Action with its more than one hundred million
dollars in money and goods since World War II witnesses im-
pressively to both the need for help and the willingness to do so.

But something is different about the situation in our time,
nonetheless. We have become conscious of the possibilities of
meeting human welfare needs through the channels of government, especially in those countries where governments are
directly responsive to the will of the people themselves. Although
the Church needs to guard against claiming too much, it is certainly true that it has been one of the powerful influences toward
this kind of general concern for human wellbeing. Government
welfare programs have become a fixed part of public policy in all
of the more highly developed countries in the world and are
increasingly being adopted as basic policy in the less developed
but rapidly rising nations.

a) The Christian will rejoice in the provisions which the
citizens of any land make for the alleviation of their real needs.
He will not be disturbed that some areas of need which were
formerly left to the Church to care for are now being provided

through public channels, even though the Church may thereby have lost a specific opportunity to bear witness to the love of God. Are there not enough needs still unmet to challenge the Christian Church? The desire to help the unfortunate has been a major force in bringing such public programs into being, and in so far as this has been the case, the Christian will applaud the motivation which lies behind them. He will, moreover, want to actively promote such programs of mutual helpfulness particularly in the less richly endowed areas of the world.

b) Christians will guard against the temptation to view such programs as any excuse for indolence or extravagance or lack of personal responsibility for one's own life and future. To look upon such programs in terms of personal profit to oneself, rather than as opportunities to contribute to the welfare of all, is to reduce them to the level of commercially profitable arrangements.

c) It cannot be denied that there is a certain risk involved for freedom in the inclination to seek security at the hands of government. The more we invoke the political order to do for us those things which it is to our advantage to do together, the more carefully we must guard against the tendency of government to extend its powers beyond our intention. There are powers that are inherent in the very nature of government. It must maintain order with justice. The Christian Church has a responsibility to help the State to understand the meaning of justice—the whole pattern of right in behalf of which government may and must properly use force to compel obedience. It is not clear that social welfare programs are inherently a part of the administration of justice. They rather constitute an arrangement for sharing risks, costs, and benefits which is handled by the State as the most inclusive unit of its citizens. There is no reason why government should not constitute the administrative unit for such inclusive welfare programs, provided only that it does not interfere with its administration of justice. The Church and the Christian will, however, recognize that such an arrangement may constitute a hazard for freedom and a temptation to those in authority to exercise powers beyond those which are intended.

5. We must speak of one more problem and issue that confronts modern Christians with a special urgency—*the problem of race relations*. There can be no basis in faith or in fact for any assumption of superiority on the part of any of God's children. The record of the more fortunate and privileged races, and in particular the white race, is compiled of sufficient injustice and oppression to give the lie to any such pretense. We have reason to be proud of and grateful for the patience and good judgment which has generally characterized the reaction of the Negro people in this country to the decision of the Supreme Court in behalf of equality. We have reason for embarrassment and shame that certain elements among the white race have not demonstrated equal qualities of character and citizenship. There is need for repentance, too, that as Christians we were not far ahead of secular authorities in abolishing the color line within our worshipping communities. The problems of race are not restricted to American soil. In Africa and Asia and the islands of the sea, wherever men are thrown together from different cultures and races, the urgency of this issue is growing by leaps and bounds. Surely no Christian will be content with any judgment about any of his neighbors which is not based on an honest effort to understand him. Christian instruction that is not global in its interest and all-inclusive in its concern cannot be Christian. There can be no lines drawn where the Christian Church is at work, either in missions, in mercy, or in learning.

There is the possibility that we have waited too long to give justice and freedom and equality to the oppressed races of the world, and that we shall not be permitted to make any great contribution or claim any credit for what is happening. Perhaps in God's providence they must themselves take the decisive steps in order that they may stand with self-respect and confidence in a new world. If that should be true, let us at least stand with bowed head, in penitence for our sins and in prayer for their success.

Each of you will know of many things that should have been said about the Christian free man's service to the world which have not been said. And perhaps this is as it should be. Christ calls to each of us as one who has been made free through His grace and points us to the world that is nearest to us. *It is there we must serve.* I would close by reminding you that it was Martin Luther who said, "For this was the reason why he put off the form of God and took on the form of a servant, that he might draw down our love for him and fasten it on our neighbor."

Bishop Friedrich Wilhelm Krummacher

Bishop Krummacher has been leader of the Evangelical Church of Pomerania in Eastern Germany for the past two years.

Born in Berlin in 1901, he is a graduate of the University of Berlin and also studied at the Universities of Tuebingen and Greifswald. He was awarded a doctorate by Tuebingen in 1927. Ordained in 1935 by the Evangelical Church of Berlin-Brandenburg, he served as vicar to Bishop Otto Dibelius, present head of this Church, (1926-28), then served a pastorate in the Ruhr district of Essen-Werden (1928-33).

He was secretary in the Foreign Office of the Evangelical Church of Germany (1933-39). Then he became a chaplain in the German army, later spending a period as a prisoner of war. After his release in 1945 he was elected general superintendent of Diocese II of the Church of Berlin-Brandenburg, which includes the East Zone of Berlin. He served there until 1955 when he was elected Bishop of Pomerania.

Free and United
in Hope

I. Not Now Yet—and Yet Even Now

OUR Lord Jesus Christ has indeed set us free; but we are still looking forward to the day of our ultimate liberation. In Christ the church is one body even now; but we are still waiting for the last day when all its divisions will be healed and He Himself will manifest its unity.

Let me begin with an experience that illustrates what I have in mind. It was several years after the end of the war, at a time when many prisoners of war were sent home. One day we were informed by our Evangelical Railway Travelers' Aid that there was a large number of pastors among those who had arrived at a certain border station. We went there at once. Now we were standing at the gate of the camp. We heard the public address system of the prison camp tell the pastors to assemble at the gate. Now we could see them come. They were still prisoners, but already they had the discharge certificate in their pocket. They were still subject to a power which even now could force them back into prison, but already they were coming home, into freedom, the camp gate was open. They were still wearing their torn prison clothes, but already they were on the way home and soon

85

would wear fresh garments. They had been living in different camp barracks, but already they were merging into a fellowship of brethren, converging toward the gate to freedom. It was a scene we shall never forget.

We are still waiting. Death and Satan still exercise their powerful influence. We have not yet been clothed with the garments of salvation (Isa. 61:10). We have not yet been united but are only isolated and hounded groups of guilt-stained people. But just the same: already we have been called out. Even now we are on the way to the glorious liberty of the sons of God. Even now we have received, in Baptism, the pledge of our deliverance. Even now the gate to freedom is opened before us.

Not now yet, and yet now already! That's why we say: "Free and united in hope." The comparison I used is, of course, inadequate and fails to reflect the fullness of divine reality; the decisive factor is missing: Christ, the Author of freedom. It is Jesus Christ who frees us; He is the living guarantee of our perfect freedom to come. He Himself calls the prisoners together into His church. He has a definite goal in view; that's why our "not yet, and yet even now" is no figment of our imagination but actual reality. Christ has snatched His church out of captivity, and now the redeemed are on the road home together, 'mid toil and tribulation still, but under the banner of our Lord Jesus Christ, the Victor.

"Free and united in hope" means that our hope is not based on some theological theory or wishful thinking; the fountain of our hope is the Lord who came down from heaven and lived as a man here on earth. Our hope rests on His incarnation and His Cross, His resurrection and His exaltation. He came once, and just as surely will come again (Rev. 1:4). He began His work, and just as surely will complete. He was able to cope with our sinful past by forgiving our sins, and just as surely will carry our redemption to its complete consummation.[1]

---

[1] This is the reason why the church, the forgiveness of our sins, and the resurrection of the dead are inseparably tied together in the third article of the Apostles' Creed.

Hence the subject that we are discussing today, Free and United in Hope, is no mere afterthought or superfluous appendix. On the contrary, all that was said here in the past week, has a direct bearing on our hope. God did not cease working on Easter or Pentecost. Release from the guilt of our sin involves the hope that eventually we shall be free from all sin and worship Him as Lord of all in everlasting innocence in union with uncounted hosts from all languages and races.

The church militant, this sinful and divided, suffering and struggling church, in which we liberated sinners are united, is marching on and has a goal: the coming kingdom of God, the church triumphant, whose head is Jesus Christ alone.

But for the present we enjoy a season of grace, we wait and hope. Under God, we still have the freedom of decision and the freedom of united service. We are living in the interval between Christ's Easter victory and His glorious return in majesty and power. Until the dawn of that great day we wait and struggle, while His ambassadors carry the message of victory (Matt. 24:14) to the ends of the earth (Acts 1:8) and to the end of time (Matt. 28:20).

II. Tokens of Victory

Some one may call us unrealistic dreamers, or enthusiasts given to wishful thinking. Oh, no; even now there are signs of victory, visible and tangible evidences that our hopes will not be shattered.

One such token of triumphant hope is *each and every church service* here on earth, even though only a handful of faithful disciples may be gathered in a catacomb, or prison camp, or in some remote corner in a country inhabited by millions of non-Christians. Each and every worship service, no matter where it is held, is a public event where the banner of victory is raised. Pastor L. Steil who died a lonely death in 1945 in the concentration camp Dachau, wrote a few weeks before his death: "Intercession before the throne of God and a deep sense of peace are the two elements that occupy my time. Tell the church everywhere that its hymns of praise to God dare never be silenced!" These victory songs, chanted by men and by angels, are strong enough to break to pieces even the most lethal weapons of political powers.

In our divine services, we voluntarily worship the Lord of the world, who though hidden, nevertheless is present, who now is known only to His church but whose visible, universal power eventually will be acknowledged by all, whether they want to or not, when He returns. Here, in the worship service, we proclaim the message that God gives redemption and freedom, and not punishment and suffering. Forgiveness of sins is bestowed on us here, now; but the freedom of the body follows only after the resurrection of the dead. Christ is really present here now, though hidden under Word and Sacrament; but on the last day His real presence will be seen by all men.[2] When we pray we are sure of the answer because the coming Lord is near us even now. Hence we pray together: "Thy kingdom come! Maranatha!" The Holy Spirit and the sacrament of Baptism are our God-given pledges of eventual victory, but God is still waging His war against the old Adam, sin, and death.[3] Since we are still living in the period of hope, every call to worship is an undeserved offer of grace. Whoever neglects the worship service will sooner or later be left without hope (Heb. 10:25). Every worship service is evidence of our unshaken hope: whatever God began to do will not remain unfinished.

The hymns of praise that we sing here on earth in any church service, even now merge with the great, heavenly doxologies recorded in the Book of Revelation (7:9ff; 19:1-8).[4] Whenever a congregation celebrates the Lord's Supper, it has a foretaste of the coming marriage supper "Until He come." He Himself, the crucified and risen Lord, gives us His Holy Supper. This communion meal—in spite of the shameful strife and separation con-

---

[2] Rev. 21:3; cf. E. Wingren, *Die Predigt,* p. 200.
[3] Cf. Luther's Small Catechism, Part IV, Question 4.
[4] Cf. Peter Brunner, *Hannover Assembly Report,* 1952, p. 58.

nected with it—is a pledge and token that the one Lord has only one body, and that He invites the members of His body to come to His table, to commune with Him and to commune with one another. The congregation, just before going to the altar, sings, "Blessed is He that cometh in the Name of the Lord." In other words, the Lord's Supper is a *praeludium regni dei,* a prelude of the perfection of the kingdom (Heb. 12:22ff).

A second victory banner of hope is raised every time Christians *practice loving service*[5] and so provide tangible proof of the message of the Gospel. The Lord who will return in glory, is the Servant of us all; that is the reason why we serve Him when we serve the brethren (Luke 12:37; Matt. 25). Service freely and regularly offered on behalf of our fellowmen keeps Christian faith from turning into something purely spiritual or intellectual. That is why we are so deeply grateful for the work of Lutheran World Service on behalf of the refugees in Hongkong, Syria, Jordan, and elsewhere. The service of Christian love is, on the one hand, a fruit of the grace bestowed on us by the Lord when He freed us and united us for such service. But on the other hand it is also a signal announcing the coming of the Lord. All our love here on earth is but imperfect and preliminary, and yearns for perfection: when will He come, He, the Fountain of life, to heal what is wounded and to establish a new earth and a new heaven! The fragmentary nature of even our best efforts constrains us to pray: "Maranatha! Even so! Come, Lord Jesus" (I Cor. 16:22; Rev. 22:10).

Loving service as a signal of the coming Lord, is an indispensable mark of the Church of Christ although the modes of service may vary. There are political and social situations where it is possible for the Church—precisely because it is waiting for the Lord to come—to help alleviate the misery of the masses and

---

[5] The German word is Diakonie; the English "diaconics" is too technical a word to be used here; other English derivatives (e.g. deacon, deaconess) from the Greek word are too specialized to be used here. What the New Testament means when using this term, is loving service, rendered for Christ's sake unselfish devotion to others without ulterior motives; unadulterated kindness to suffering fellowmen, genuine stewardship of time, talents, possessions, and self.

perhaps exercise its influence so that the laws of the land are applied with equity and fairness or if need be improved. Wherever possible Christians ought to do their share toward making living conditions here on earth more peaceful, just and humane; for this earth—though it does not know it yet—belongs to the Lord of peace and justice, truth and mercy.

But even in such situations where the church has been deprived of a place in public life, it nevertheless faces the duty to exercise loving service. In many cases—in a filthy prison cell, or behind the barbed wire of a concentration camp, for instance, when a man shares his last crust of dry bread with a hungry fellow prisoner instead of eating it himself—a simple act of love is much more effective than many fine words. The coming Lord victorious in whom we hope and who will some day establish His glorious rule, walks among us even now, hidden among the lowly and crushed, the dispossessed, the refugees and the persecuted, the "least of His brethren." Even the plainest deed of loving service is a taken of hope. Our despised Lord Himself has said that the time will come when He will order all nations to appear before His royal throne and say to them, "Truly, I say to you, as you did it to one of the least of these my brethren, you did it to me" (Matt. 25:31-40). When the Lord returns to assume His kingdom He will pronounce the final verdict concerning the service that every one has rendered (Rev. 22:12). That is why it is necessary, even now, to recognize the coming Victor and King in the guise of our hungering and suffering brethren.

A third token of hope triumphant is the *missionary witness throughout the world.* Not as though we imagined that our own missionary zeal could bring about the Christianization of the world in our generation; we labor no longer under such optimistic illusions. The notion that the old churches of Europe and America are the determining agents in the work of missions and the people of Asia and Africa mere objects, has lost its basis since we have come into personal contact with the young churches. Nevertheless, our missionary witness is a signal of eventual victory wherever the church of Jesus Christ functions exclusively as a never-ceasing Christ-initiated missionary movement—at home within its own nation and abroad in ecumenical fellowship with sister churches. Reflecting on what the Bible says about the church's mission we have learned to speak very humbly about our own part: our Lord Jesus Christ invariably viewed the work of world missions from an eschatological aspect. It is only when He returns that all nations—also Israel—will be assembled at His holy mountain.[6]

And yet, each and every time our missionary witness invades the domain of the demons, of the dethroned deities, or of militant atheism, we have a *foretaste of the sure victory* of the Lord to come; it is a partial realization of His ultimate total victory in the world. When the church—conquering the temptations of pious self-admiration and facile syncretism—boldly assumes its missionary obligation; when it refuses to be cooped up, like a domestic animal, in a circumscribed ghetto-like sphere; when ordinary Christians publicly give their plain witness in their daily life—in all such instances the Lord, despised and unknown though He be, is proclaimed as the Lord of all lords, as the coming Lord of all men and all nations. He is able to secure for Himself all the rooms He needs even as once He found room in the cradle and on the cross (II Tim. 2:9).

The Church's missionary witness to the coming Lord is also a source of *abiding comfort* in view of all those many things in the church's history that are left incomplete or have crumbled to pieces and have been swept away by the hurricane of world history. We have this comfort even when we think of whole churches that once were thriving and flourishing and then disappeared; we need to mention only the church of North Africa fifteen hundred years ago, or the Evangelical Churches east of the Oder river in our own day. These churches, though crushed

---

[6] Rom. 11:12ff; Isa. 2:2-3; Micah 4:1ff; Mark 13:10; cf. Jeremias, *Jesu Verheissung fuer die Voelker* 1956.

and exterminated, have performed their important historical service and, though dead, are yet living signals of the Lord who will come when all our church work will be gone and forgotten. Even our defeats, individual or collective, for instance in our struggle against the onrush of Islam or modern atheism, yes even the unseen, unknown martyrdom of a lonely sufferer in a prison cell—they all reflect the shining radiance of the rising Sun of righteousness, the Lord of light (Mal. 4:2; II Thess. 1:4-5). The coming Lord unites us all in the fellowship of intercession, even those who are quite isolated from the rest of us, for instance in Siberia or China, and on a larger scale, also the minority or diaspora churches, scattered here and there among the nations; they all are precious "seedgrains of hope" (Zech. 10:9; Acts 8:4).

The mission of the church travels the same road as its crucified King; the two are inseparably united. And though to human eyes the Cross is nothing but inglorious defeat, to us it is the hallowed token of inevitable victory.

III. Service and Suffering in the Light of Hope

Looking forward to the coming of the Lord cures us of the illusion as though by our activity we might be able to change the world into a kind of paradise. The Lord Himself, the Lord of glory, has reserved for Himself the consummation of our deliverance and the establishment of His rule. That is why we must never think of church institutions as ends in themselves though they may be very necessary as the means by which we carry out our service in this world. Our brethren in the young churches, therefore, are free to shape and arrange their own church life as they themselves see fit. And we who live in countries ruled by Communism and are aware of the radical changes of our social conditions, have the duty as well as the freedom, soberly to examine the question whether or not the traditional parochial system of the folk-church should be superseded by new forms of free and active congregations ready to witness and if need be

92

to battle. We do not mean to be ungrateful for the missionary opportunities which the folk-church system has given us and still gives us; we know, however, that the future does not belong to any one traditional form of the church, but only to the Lord Himself.

Each and every Christian is called upon, in office and workshop, at home and in church, to witness of the Lord to whom the future belongs. Not the least part of this witness is that we serve the Lord Jesus Christ by freely *confessing* Him, with our own lips, before our fellowmen; pagans and atheists are often more ready to listen to the testimony of a layman than when we preach from our pulpits. This service, too, is rendered with a view to the return of the Lord who on the last day will require us to give an account of our stewardship (Luke 16:2). Those who bow their knees to the Lord who gave them their freedom, will never bow down to the lords and powers of this world.

But when the church boldly witnesses of its hope in the Crucified as the coming Lord of all, the world will surely raise its voice in opposition because it puts its trust in other lords and powers. There is no way for a church that acknowledges the unseen Lord to be the Ruler of the universe and serves Him alone, to avoid suffering and persecution here on earth. *Affliction and persecution* obviously was the normal situation of the apostles (I Cor. 4:12-13; II Cor. 6:4f; 11:23ff; Rev. 13:10). A church that carries the designation "holy and apostolic" ought to be amazed and even terrified if its course here on earth is smooth and unobstructed. Luther, at any rate, thought that suffering was a "genuine mark of the early church."[7] Christians who bear the cross while they are on the way to meet their Lord, should be less afraid of affliction and suffering than of the individual temptation to conform in their church life to the outward splendor of this world.

Suffering leads to *repentance:* how often have we not given the wrong kind of offence to our persecutors! And it leads to stronger

[7] Luther, *Wider Hans Worst* 1541.

hope in the Lord (Rev. 1:9). Keeping its eyes fixed unwaveringly on the Lord to come, a church in the state of persecution will be able to avoid these three forms of hopelessness:

defeatism, i.e., a resigned retreat into the ghetto of quietistic inwardness;

compromise, i.e., adopting certain elements of man-made religions or ideologies for the sake of a foul peace;

purely negative political resistance, sadly deploring the loss of the social systems of a past age and forgetting that the Lord of history is and remains the Crucified One who uses no other means but Word and Sacrament until He reveals His great power on the last day.

But where the altars of *substitute religions* are erected or where an earthly paradise is promised in the place of the Christian hope for the coming of the Lord, there Christians today face the same situation as the early Christians, who refused to offer incense to Caesar and said, "We must obey God rather than men" (Acts 5:29).

In such situations the church will experience anew that seasons of tribulation, oppression, and even bloody persecution may be especially blessed and profitable (I Pet. 4:14, 15). The cross borne by the church reflects the glory of Christ. Where Christians suffer for Christ's sake, the situation is never hopeless but, on the contrary, full of promise because in the midst of such suffering the light of Christ's glory shines brightly. According to Luther, "hope is always on the increase; suffering and persecution make it grow."[8] Those who disregard the threats of men and keep witnessing of Christ even when it leads into tribulation and pain, enjoy even now the blessed assurance of Christ's eschatological promise, "Whosoever shall confess me before him, him will I confess also before my Father who is in heaven" (Matt. 10:32). Young people, fourteen year old confirmands among us have experienced the truth of this promise when they had to choose between Christian confirmation and atheistic "youth-consecra-

---

[8] Luther, *Advent Postil* 1522.

94

tion." When Christ frees a man, He frees him also from cowardice.

It has been the experience of the church that the Lord, now and then, grants it a period of refreshing, as it were, a breathing space when it may work quietly at its tasks. Church history shows that God ever and again opens up new opportunities for the preaching of the Gospel even when doors are closing. We are never fighting for a lost cause even if our present church forms should have to be discontinued. The persecutions on the island of Madagascar have brought forth wonderful and permanent fruits in the form of lay activity and revival movements. The same testimony is given us by our brethren in Ethiopia: the persecutions from 1935 to 1941 resulted in greatly increased lay activity and evangelism.[9] We too have been permitted to observe this connection between persecution and revival in the heavily decimated evangelical congregations east of the Oder river, where since the days of the Reformation there existed a flourishing evangelical church-life and now since 12 years there are only a few faithful lay preachers left, men and women, to gather the scattered church members around Word and Sacrament while the large majority of the inhabitants are either communists or Roman Catholics.

It is a great comfort for the waiting church that the glory of the coming Lord is even now reflected in His suffering members. This does not mean that the oppressed and persecuted members of the body of Christ should be pitied; on the contrary, they have been given the honor of serving as the *vanguard of hope,* running to meet the Lord (Mark 13:13; Matt. 16:24-27). Pain, suffering, persecution are some of the means by which the Lord unites His church; this is one of our own really heart-cheering experiences of the past few years: the fellowship of suffering and pain, of intercession and help across chasms of ideological and political differences. "If one member suffers, all suffer together" (I Cor. 12:26). Suffering ever rekindles the flame of the church's

---

[9] Marangu, *Record*, p. 154.160.

hope and keeps it from being snuffed out. Tribulations rouse the church to witness and, if need be, even to martyrdom. This witness is today, as always, a seed of hope. "Here is the call for the endurance and faith of the saints" (Rev. 13:10). In affliction and pain the unity of the church actualizes itself in the common prayer, "Maranatha. Even so. Come, Lord Jesus." And that is why we *praise* God for allowing afflictions to come upon His church (II Cor. 1:3-5).

IV. *Christ the Victor*

When we speak of Christ we speak of His body. When we speak of the body of Christ, we speak of the head of the body, Christ (Rom. 12:5). When we speak of justification by faith, we speak of Christ. When we speak of Christ, we speak of the church composed of justified sinners. In spite of all the divisions —and we are often ashamed of them—the church is one because it has one Lord.

He is the one good Shepherd and He will gather His scattered flock at His return (Jer. 23:2; John 10:16), we know. Nevertheless, we Christians who hope in His coming, have the commission, even now, tangibly and authentically, to demonstrate that this unity is here because the one Lord is here who has freed us all in the same way, for life in one and the same fellowship. The obligation to actualize church unity rests especially heavy on us when we think of the young churches; we ought to examine our proclamation of the Gospel with reference to its "offensive" elements and discard those among them which are not genuine and only hinder our missionary service, and we ought to remove our divisions, at least as far as our fidelity to the apostolic truth permits. That is why we are so grateful for the tokens of our Lord's victory in the growing fellowship of the ecumenical movement today. Here, too, is a prelude to the never ceasing hymns of adoration sung by the people of God in honor of the Lamb (Rev. 19:1ff; 21:22ff).

In view of the Lord's return we, the redeemed and united members of Christendom, are called upon even now to have the unshakable assurance of His victory and to draw the practical consequences from it. True, we dare not anticipate His victory and act as though the battle were over; we are permitted to hear the message of victory but not to see it with our eyes. And it may well happen that God leads His people into even deeper anguish, as we approach the end of time; Holy Writ speaks of wide-spread apostasy in the church and many terrifying and hideous trials to come.

And yet: *the victory has been won*. The Victor is on the way to meet us, to liberate us for good. Some of us know from actual experience the truth and aptness of Luther's magnificent illustration: a prisoner, chained in the dungeon, but in full confidence, is waiting for the moment of his rescue; the troops of his lord are already attacking the castle; the castle is already going up in flames; the noise of battle grows louder as the fighting grows fiercer; disorder and horror increase; the odor of death is all around; smoke fills the air; the prisoner sees nothing but—he knows that his lord is coming and will be there soon. The more ghastly the battle, the closer and the surer the victory! This is the road the Savior leads His church.

"Blessed are those servants whom the Master finds awake when He comes" (Luke 12:37).

Preface to the Theses

The Third Assembly of the Lutheran World Federation which was held in Minneapolis, August 15-25, 1957, sends Christian greetings to all Lutheran congregations in the world. Our hearts are filled with gratitude and joy. We are grateful to God for the rich blessings which He granted us throughout these days. It is with joy and affection that we think of the fellowship with so many brethren and sisters from all over the world.

We have been meeting in a time of perplexities and hidden fears. We have realized the alarming signs of a new catastrophe which, if it would happen, would be far more destructive than anything mankind has ever seen before. We have tried to face the intellectual problems and the spiritual needs of men today. We have recognized in all humility that the Church, too, has been affected by the growing uncertainty, by lack of faith and love. Even in those countries which owe their best spiritual heritage to the Christian faith, materialism and moral disintegration have become an acute danger.

In the face of this world situation we desire to reaffirm our faith in Jesus Christ who frees us and unites us. We state our conviction that the solution of the grave problems of our day is not to be found in social, scientific or political programs only, but in the promises which God has given to His people in Jesus Christ. They are valid not only for the life to come but also for the life in this world.

We have given our thoughts and prayers to the task of reconsidering our faith in view of this situation. Twenty discussion groups have engaged in this process of thinking together. The result of this work is summarized in the following theses.

We hand them over to all Lutheran congregations in the world, to their pastors, teachers, and members. We thank you for your prayers, which have been with us throughout all these days. We ask you to give these theses your prayerful study and careful consideration. It is our hope that they may inspire Christians all over the world, and that they may lead them to a new understanding of the riches of our faith and to a deeper loyalty to our Lord.

BISHOP HANNS LILJE

I. The Freedom We Have in Christ

1

We praise God the Creator, the fountain of all life, Who made man in His own image, and who in Jesus Christ has come to set us free.

2

The magnificence of the Creator's endowment of his creature imparts richness and fullness to man's search for freedom and unity. Man's culture is the form his productive vitality takes as he variously unfolds this endowment.

But every achievement of man within his creaturely existence is both perverted and ambiguous; for the freedom and unity bestowed by the Creator is corrupted by man's fractured God-relationship. In the Scriptures God reveals the name and truth of this situation to be sin. Guilt, captivity by demonic powers, death are the results of it.

3

This means that human freedom and unity, as envisioned and achieved by man, is both restless and full of pathos: restless because the creature is not abandoned by the Creator; pathetic because every achievement denies the original endowment. Unless, therefore, the right God-relationship is restored men can be neither free nor united. Fear, anxiety, wretchedness are the marks of man's existence. Man is formed by God for freedom and unity; and he is bound within the limitations of his broken humanity.

4

Man is not able to restore his life in relation to God. Because he cannot do so, he cannot achieve true order, lasting peace, or fulfillment in any other relationship. His effort to do so but confirms the desperate nature of his plight. The very forms in which he struggles toward earthly freedom and unity become occasions for the demonic: social solidarity tempts to idolatry, power tempts to tyranny, mastery tempts to pride. Man is this predicament needs the Deliverer who is more powerful than everything that is wrong; and deliverance needs to take place where wrongness reigns. God alone can free, and God alone can unite; and He unites by freeing.

5

This deliverance is accomplished because God in Christ invaded man's predicament. He became WHAT man is WHERE man is. For our sake He, who knew no sin, was made sin for us so that we might become righteous before God. The Son of God stood in the place where guilty man stands. He confronted the onslaught of the demonic powers, and overcame them. He died our death, and He conquered death.

6

The liberation which God once for all accomplished in the incarnation, life, death, resurrection and exaltation of Jesus Christ, He bestows and makes effective even now and forever.

7

What God did in the desolation of the cross is received by faith and in the brokenness of repentance. As man's situation is illumined before the cross, so there, too, his righteousness is judged and God's righteousness is imparted.

8

In the church man is grasped by the Gospel, incorporated into this redemptive action of God in baptism, and revitalized and sustained by the power of the Holy Spirit. So crucial is this renewal of life that the resurrection of the Lord is alone adequate to create and describe it. "We know that we have passed out of death into life" (I John 3:14).

9

Faith begins with what God does; it is trust that God will accomplish what He promises; it is man's life in the faithfulness of God. His faithfulness begets man's faith. "If God is for us, who is against us!" (Romans 8:31.)

10

Much is against us: the limitations of our broken humanity, the enigmas of history, the pride of our religiousness, death-dealing choices in practical ethics. But what God has done drives into all of this with His action of forgiveness and the restoration of the new being in Christ. Whoever, in all of this can say, "Abba, Father," has indeed the gift of freedom.

11

The freedom we have in Christ is actual for it is GIVEN—"Where the spirit of the Lord is, there IS freedom" (II Corinthians 3:17). This freedom is received and lived out within the limitations of history. But the giver and guarantor of this freedom is God; therefore, we wait in hope, "For in this hope we were saved" (Romans 8:24).

II. The Unity of the Church in Christ

1

Men reconciled to God are one in Jesus Christ. Charged with the ministry and the message of reconciliation, the church herself is the first-fruit of reconciliation: by baptism we are made a people with a life together, a communion, a body, the body of Christ.

2

Thus her unity is found and founded in Jesus Christ. Neither by ideals nor by enthusiasm, neither by tolerance nor by agreements, are we made one—but by Jesus Christ. In all our attempts to manifest the unity of the church in visible church fellowship, the dimensions should be neither smaller nor greater than the dimensions Christ has given His church.

3

As the communion of reconciliation the church suffers under her dividedness. We may find some consolation but no excuse in referring to an invisible unity of all true believers. We know that the ministry of reconciliation is jeopardized by the lack of manifested unity.

4

In this situation the Lutheran churches are called back to their confession: "To the true unity of the church it is enough to agree concerning the doctrine of the Gospel and the administration of the Sacraments; nor is it necessary that human traditions, that is rites or ceremonies instituted by man, should be everywhere alike." Here the words "It is enough" witness to our freedom: Wherever we hear the Gospel preached in its truth and purity and see the Sacraments administered according to the institution of Christ, there we may be assured that the one Church of Christ is present. There nothing separates us from our brethren, and both faith and love constrain us to overcome our dividedness.

5

For our Lutheran churches with a diverse past and different situations and commitments in the present, this "it is enough" transcends local, national and synodical traditions and urges us to express our unity at the Lord's table where we partake of the one Body.

6

The words "it is enough" give the Lutheran churches a freedom also in relation to other churches. Bound by them we are led to the Scriptures and so rescued from the pressures of institutional expediency as well as from complacent acceptance of the status quo. In an ecumenical study of the Scriptures we find the most hopeful means towards a fuller realization of the unity in Christ and towards a deeper understanding of our faith as found in and behind our confessional statements. On this basis also the questions of inter-communion and the nature of the Sacraments can be brought out of the present deadlock. For our Lutheran churches, it is a congenial and timely task to participate in and initiate such ecumenical studies —on the highest theological, as well as on the parish level.

7

God reconciled the world unto himself. Jew and Gentile, slave and free, man and woman were made one in Christ; this event has affected social life and customs, legislation and economic life, and has given the world a new zeal for overcoming human divisions. Sometimes the incentive of the Gospel proves effective even when the churches keep silent or resist its implications. We should rejoice in the influence of the Gospel wherever and whenever it appears. Yet, since our unity is deeply rooted in what Christ wrought, it must be nurtured by faith in Him and thus redeemed from becoming re-enslaved under the demonic elements in nationalism, materialism and secularism.

8

Where the concern for overcoming human divisions in this world meets what appears to be insurmountable difficulties, the church is especially called to her ministry of reconciliation, asking for the power of the Holy Spirit to add the witness of life to the message she has in its Gospel. In so doing the church is not performing a service alien to her essential life; she witnesses by being what she is: the communion of those reconciled.

9

While the Kingdom of God in its fullness is yet to come when all things are united in Christ, we are called to pray and act according to the words of our Lord: Thy will be done on earth as it is in heaven.

III. The Freedom to Reform the Church

1

Through all ages there is one holy catholic and apostolic church, whose head is Jesus Christ. In Him the Father was revealed and to Him the Holy Spirit bears witness guiding us into all the truth.

2

The church as the pilgrim people of God is being led toward the full realization of the Kingdom of God. In her life on the way, she has her promise and her temptation. The promise is that the Lord will abide with her even to the end of the age and the gates of hell shall not prevail against her. The temptation is to betray her only Lord.

3

This temptation manifests itself in many ways. On the one hand, the church is tempted to glorify herself as the Kingdom of God which is to come, to equate her own words with the Word of God, her theological statements about Christ with the living Lord Himself, the repetition of venerable confessions with living confession. On the other hand, the church is tempted to distort the proclamation of the crucified and risen Lord as her only Savior and King into political and economic ideologies, religious syncretism, self-sufficient moralism, or individual sentimentalities in order to make her message acceptable to man.

4

From the very beginning the church was called to be the herald of the truth, receiving and delivering the apostolic message of the mighty deeds of God in the history of salvation, supremely the life and earthly ministry, death, and resurrection of Jesus Christ, and calling men to repentance and faith. This apostolic tradition in which the living Lord Himself reigns and acts, remains sovereign and unchangeable throughout all ages. In every generation the church must be confronted and judged by this apostolic message. This is her ongoing reformation.

5

Reformation, therefore, is not creation of a new church but recovery of the true church. Reformation is not a revolt against the authentic tradition but a protest against human traditions in the church which pervert the Gospel of Christ. Reformation is not itching eagerness for novelty, but a penitent and obedient subjection to the renewing Spirit.

6

The Lutheran church declares her witness to be continuous with the ecumenical creeds and affirms in faith and joyful thanksgiving the recovery of the true marks of the church by the reformation.

7

The Lutheran confessions claim our allegiance because they not only proclaimed the Gospel in a crucial age of the church's life in accordance with the Scriptures, but they continue to direct us in our understanding of the Scriptures consistent with apostolic tradition.

8

Listening obediently to the Scriptures, abiding in the apostolic tradition, and free to respond to the demands of our time, the church trusts the Holy Spirit to guide her to confess her faith rightly and relevantly in continuity with her historic witness.

9

Churches in Asia and Africa face an urgent challenge to relate the Christian message to the needs of a world of resurgent non-Christian religions and to develop an indigenous form of church life. In performing this task, they are free and obliged in the same obedience and continuity, to assume the burden of responsible confession in their own time and place.

10

The church is called to enter into the life of each age, to penetrate its thinking, to feel with it in its excitements and torments, and thus to administer God's healing power with precision and compassion. For her obedience to be effective, the church must boldly face the massive revolutionary facts of our time. Among these are anti-Christian ideologies, political turmoil, social rootlessness, ethical relativism, the issues raised by scientific methodology and the world-wide resurgence of non-Christian or pseudo-Christian religiosity.

11

In this situation the church cannot be content with timid lamentations. She must pray for the gift of the Holy Spirit that she may be empowered with humility, wisdom and courage. This is her promised renewal.

IV. Free for Service in the World

1

Christ came to the world as a servant. Justified by Him through faith, we are made free to serve one another by love, and he to whom much is forgiven, loves much. Christian faith is active in love. "Our Lord put off the form of God and took on the form of a servant, that He might draw down our love for Him and fasten it on our neighbor" (Luther).

2

As God's commandments are grounded in His loving concern for mankind, so there can be no genuine law and social justice without love—and true love for our fellow men leads to a concern for social, political, and economic justice.

3

In her concern for love and justice the church may not identify herself with any one political, social, or economic system. She calls men and nations under whatever system to act responsibly before God and His law.

4

Thus we are called to translate love and compassion into the structures of justice. In matters of civil liberties and racial integration, of

113

concern for the uprooted and for people in areas of rapid social change, and of care for the mentally and physically disabled, our love fails if it does not materialize in recognition of human rights.

5

Where justice falls short in the complexities and the brokenness of our human endeavors, there especially the Christian finds his calling to follow his Lord in service and suffering. Freed by Christ and quickened by the Holy Spirit, he exercises the inventiveness of love.

6

Made free to serve in the world, we are also redeemed from the pressures of conformity. God's Word often questions what our environment takes for granted; the Spirit gives us the courage to stand alone. Through the church He gives us the means to join in spirit and action where the individual could accomplish little. In worship as well as in united efforts to meet man's need, all lives are given meaning and purpose.

7

In and through our calling we serve God. The process by which a believer applies the Word of God to his everyday work should be recognized as a painstaking task. If it is not so considered, we accept the status quo without question and allow the social and political development to proceed independent of the Word of God. The more complex or the more meaningless our work appears, the greater is the duty of the church to help its members to a mature faith and a realistic insight into the facts and structures of this world. This requires instruction as well as imagination. Imagination requires freedom; this freedom Christ gives when He frees us to serve our fellow men.

8

Jesus Christ healed the sick and restored joy to the despised. This was but a prelude to and a token of His great service, when He gave His life a ransom for many. With this Gospel, the church serves the world in its basic need and plight. Such service, having its origin in Christ, cannot rest until the word of salvation has been received. Yet, our service of love does not depend on a response nor is it motivated by strategic considerations. It is a love which does not ask for results.

V. Free and United
in Hope

1

The church lives by faith in Jesus Christ. Her hope is centered in Him, the risen Lord. She knows Him as the one who came and established His kingdom. She knows Him as her Lord here and now who rules the world with sovereign power. She knows Him as the King who will come in glory as Judge and Savior.

2

The church lives by the salvation Christ wrought; not in nostalgic retrospection towards a golden past—neither that of Jesus' earthly ministry nor that of any great period of church history—but with her eyes open toward the future, in joyful anticipation of the coming of Christ and His kingdom.

3

When the church speaks about hope she does not witness to the truth of human optimism or assess its value—nor does she endorse human pessimism as more true to fact. She does not engage in dreams about a "Christianized world." The Christian hope is not a religiously strengthened cheerfulness but takes hold of the promises of God, rejoices in their fulfillment in the resurrection of Jesus Christ and looks forward to their consummation.

4

The Christian hope is more than hopefulness. It is anticipation of the kingdom, which has drawn near with the gift of the Spirit, the "downpayment" of our inheritance. Thus the Spirit is not merely a guarantee for the future, but a power for the present.

5

This power and this hope manifest themselves most clearly in the essential activities of the church: worship, mission and service to our fellow men. Each of them is a token of victory.

6

In the Sacrament of Baptism we are brought under the power of His resurrection and are born anew to a living hope, waiting for the redemption of our bodies. In His Word God acts here and now as our Judge and Savior. The Sacrament of the Altar, where Christ is really present, is the anticipation of the heavenly banquet. He who comes to us in bread and wine, is the same Christ, who is to come in glory.

7

The mission of the church as a work in the power of the Holy Spirit is independent of human hopefulness and disillusionment. Whenever the witness to the Gospel invades the domain of demonic powers, idolatry and militant or creeping atheism, the ultimate victory of the Lord is foreshadowed.

8

Serving our fellow men, diakonia, is hope engaged in its proper business, especially needed where human hopes are running low. Such service is not a second thought following our devotion to Christ. It is a manifestation of His kingdom and a token of His victory over all powers of destruction.

9

In all these matters the power is that of the Spirit of Jesus Christ who was glorified through a cross. Because of His cross we look forward to the Day of the Lord with victorious joy and penitent trembling. Through the cross the church recognizes the judgment of her human hopes and receives the power and hope of the Holy Spirit.

10

Hope is a glorious "must" for a church under pressure and persecution. The hope of the church is most alive when it suffers most. The church which enjoys the good will of its surroundings is often threatened in its spiritual integrity. The dimension of hope is the dimension of the Spirit.

11

Therefore the church has to be cleansed from all that would transform the manifestations of the kingdom into human activities of a society for the preservation and promotion of Christianity as a philosophy, an ideology, or a way of living. It is only in the dimension of hope and with the power of the Spirit that the church can be true to herself and her Lord.

12

In Christ we are free and one. The Holy Spirit quickens our imagination, arouses our courage, sobers our wishfulness, strengthens our patience. When God's Spirit witnesses with our spirit about the consummation of His kingdom, He calls us to make manifest the freedom and the unity we have in Christ.